SEVENTH EDITION

Hockey NOW!

MIKE LEONETTI

A Gift of **READING**

Mrs. Butt & 7-2

A Gift For

Anonymous 2013

From   Year

SCHOLASTIC
Read Every Day. Lead a Better Life.

FIREFLY BOOKS

A FIREFLY BOOK

Published by Firefly Books Ltd. 2012

First printing

Publisher Cataloging-in-Publication Data (U.S.)
Leonetti, Mike, 1958-
     Hockey now! / Mike Leonetti.
7th ed.
[176] p. : col. ill. ; cm.
Includes index.
ISBN-13: 978-1-77085-105-4 (pbk.)
1. National Hockey League -- Biography. 2. Hockey players -- Biography. I. Title.
796.962/0922 B dc23   GV848.5.A1.L466 2012

Library and Archives Canada Cataloguing in Publication
Leonetti, Mike, 1958-
          Hockey now! / Mike Leonetti. -- 7th ed.
Includes index.
ISBN 978-1-77085-105-4
1. Hockey players--Biography. 2. National Hockey League--Biography. 3. Hockey players--Pictorial works. 4. National Hockey League--Pictorial works. I. Title.
GV848.5.A1L455 2012   796.962092'2   C2012-902184-9

Published in the United States by
Firefly Books (U.S.) Inc.
P.O. Box 1338, Ellicott Station
Buffalo, New York 14205

Published in Canada by
Firefly Books Ltd.
66 Leek Crescent
Richmond Hill, Ontario L4B 1H1

Cover and interior design: Kimberley Young

Printed in Canada

The publisher gratefully acknowledges the financial support for our publishing program by the Government of Canada through the Canada Book Fund as administered by the Department of Canadian Heritage.

PHOTO CREDITS

DEDICATION

The seventh edition of *Hockey Now!* is dedicated to all the members of the Los Angeles Kings organization who won their first ever Stanley Cup in 2012 after being an NHL member club since the 1967–68 season.

CONTENTS

INTRODUCTION

When Nicklas Lidstrom of the Detroit Red Wings called it a career at the end of the 2011–12 season, it marked the end of a phenomenal run for one of the best defensemen to ever play in the NHL. Over our seven editions of *Hockey Now!*, we have had the pleasure of documenting the careers of some of the best to ever play the game. Legends like Wayne Gretzky, Joe Sakic, Ray Bourque, Mario Lemieux and Mats Sundin have all graced the pages of this almanac through the years, and as each one retired we bid them congratulations and a fond farewell.

Over Lidstrom's 20-year NHL career he has made himself a legend in the mold of those before him, defined by consistency and otherworldly excellence. He skated in 1,564 games, totaled 1,142 points and posted a fabulous plus-450 rating. He won four Stanley Cups, seven James Norris Memorial Trophies and one Conn Smythe Trophy; he was twice selected to the Second All-Star Team and was selected for the First All-Star Team an incredible 10 times. If he decided to play the 2012–13 season, he would have made his 7th appearance in *Hockey Now!* — tying him with Martin Brodeur for the most appearances of any player. For that, we'd like to salute the Swedish-born defenseman's Hall of Fame–worthy career.

A Nicklas Lidstrom–caliber player isn't made overnight, and there are many stars featured in this book that are coming into their prime years with career trajectories that look promising. These stars, players like Sidney Crosby, Evgeni Malkin, Henrik Lundqvist, Jonathan Toews, Alex Ovechkin and Steven Stamkos, are the leaders of the game as it stands today, and the expectation is that they should excel as league leaders for years to come. When they do decide to leave the game, the hope is that they will do so with as glowing a résumé as Lidstrom's.

Not many players are able to compete at the NHL level for 20 years, as Lidstrom did, and furthermore, not many are able to be a star performer into their 40s. However, there is one player, the incomparable Martin Brodeur, who turned 40 in 2012, and he leads a crop of superstar veterans found within the pages of *Hockey Now!* including: Jarome Iginla, Brad Richards, Zdeno Chara, Ilya Kovalchuk and Pavel Datsyuk. These players give their teams veteran leadership that they can count on every night, and they will surely make up a large part of a future class of Hall of Fame nominations.

As young players continue to enter the league, new stars are discovered every year. Players featured in *Hockey Now!* on the verge of stardom include: Taylor Hall, Claude Giroux, Pekka Rinne, Erik Karlsson, Jonathan Quick, Drew Doughty, Evander Kane, Max Pacioretty, Logan Couture, Jake Gardiner, Tyler Seguin and Alex Pietrangelo, among many others. These players exhibit the skill, speed and talent that typifies the modern NHL.

Today's players can shoot the puck harder and move it more quickly than at any time in NHL history. Their play-making skills are a sight to behold when they are allowed to display their obvious talents. The game of hockey works best when the top talent is asked to play a two-way game. It can be done, and the players presented in the following pages reflect the most explosive, talent-rich crop of players ever featured in *Hockey Now!*

Enjoy!

Mike Leonetti

EASTERN CONFERENCE TEAM STARS

The best of the Atlantic, Northeast and Southeast.

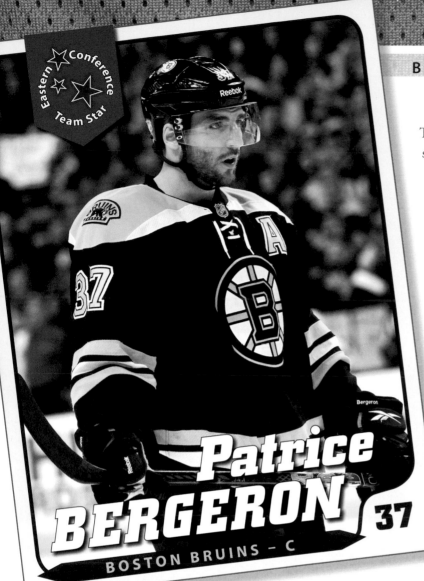

Patrice BERGERON 37
BOSTON BRUINS – C

The two teams split the next two contests to force a seventh and deciding game in Vancouver the night of June 15, 2011. Boston's road team had lost every game up to this point in the series. In order to win Game 7 on the Canucks' home ice, the Bruins would need a big effort from their best forward and faceoff specialist Patrice Bergeron.

Bergeron didn't disappoint. Late in the first period, with the score knotted at zero, he redirected a pass behind Canucks netminder Roberto Luongo for the lead. It turned out that was all the Bruins would need. After Boston scored another goal to make it 2–0, a penalty call to the Bruins threatened to give Vancouver some life, but Bergeron put any thoughts of a Canuck comeback to rest by breaking away to score a shorthanded goal. It was not the prettiest — it had to be reviewed — but his effort to get down the ice with a defenseman on his back was the stuff of sheer determination. The puck somehow skittered and bounced past Luongo, but what it lacked in grace it made up for in impact.

The goal completely flattened the Canucks, and the Bruins went on to claim the Stanley Cup with a 4–0 victory.

Bergeron had not scored in the Stanley Cup final until this game, but his two goals could not have come at a more opportune time. His final totals for the 2011 playoffs were six goals and 14 assists for 20 points in 23 hard-fought games. Bergeron was also amazing at the dot, winning over 60 percent of his draws and having the best record of anyone to take more than 120 faceoffs (he took 497). His great effort in Game 7 of the 2011 final helped complete a great comeback for Bergeron, whose career had nearly ended after being hit from behind a few years earlier.

On the night of October 27, 2007, just 10 games into the 2007–08 season, Bergeron was hit into the boards squarely from behind during a game against the Philadelphia Flyers. The crushing blow sent Bergeron down to the ice immediately, and he did not move for

The Boston Bruins did not have an easy time advancing to the 2011 Stanley Cup final. It took them seven games to dispatch their rivals from Montreal, and another seven games to do away with the Tampa Bay Lightning. In between those two series the Bruins won an impressive and emotional four-game sweep of the Philadelphia Flyers. That series was payback for the collapse they suffered the year previous when Philadelphia came from a three games to nothing deficit to oust Boston in Game 7.

The Stanley Cup final featured the big, bad Bruins against the Presidents' Trophy–winning Vancouver Canucks. The Bruins quickly found themselves down two games to zero in Vancouver after a pair of one-goal losses before going back home to Boston to tie the series.

quite some time before being carried off on a stretcher. He suffered a severe concussion and missed the rest of the season.

With post-concussion syndrome hampering the simplest of tasks, the talented center's hockey career appeared to be in jeopardy. Bergeron had to fight nausea and constant headaches and much of his day was spent lying down in a dark room. This went on for months, until the 22 year old returned to NHL play for 64 games in the 2008–09 season. Unfortunately, Bergeron was not the same productive player he had previously been. He scored a mere eight goals that season and rarely played like the 18 year old he'd been when he joined the league right out of junior hockey. Thankfully, with time and youth on his side, Bergeron was eventually able to recapture much of his old form.

Bergeron proved he was recovering his touch with a 19-goal season in 2009–10, a year that also saw him play as a faceoff and shutdown specialist for Team Canada at the 2010 Winter Olympics. In fact, Bergeron's post-concussion career has focused more on being a two-way,

shutdown player.

The 2010–11 campaign saw him score 22 times and set up 35 helpers for a total of 57 points in 80 games while posting a plus-20 rating.

The 2011–12 season saw Bergeron's strong play continue with a 64-point, plus-36 rating campaign in 81 contests. Bergeron's impressive comeback gives hope to all those who long to return to the game they love after suffering a serious injury.

CAREER HIGHLIGHTS

➤ Drafted 45th overall by the Boston Bruins in 2003

➤ Scored Stanley Cup–winning goal versus the Vancouver Canucks in 2011 final

➤ Posted a league-best plus-36 mark in 2011–12

➤ Named winner of the Frank J. Selke Trophy in 2012

➤ Recorded 143 goals and 401 points in 537 career games

Eastern Conference Team Star

Ryan MILLER 30

BUFFALO SABRES – G

ticularly bad. It seemed unfair that Miller had to keep bearing all that was wrong with the Buffalo team, and to make matters worse, his season took a dive in November when, while attempting to play the puck outside of his crease in a game in Boston, he was needlessly run over by 6-foot-4, 220-pound Boston Bruins forward Milan Lucic. Miller swung his stick at Lucic but didn't make any significant contact. The hit, however, gave the goaltender a concussion and knocked him from the lineup for nine games. The Sabres went 3–5–1 over that stretch, which helped to dig an early hole that ultimately hurt Buffalo's chances of getting into the playoffs.

After his experience with Lucic's hit, Miller's already steady voice as a hockey-safety advocate only got louder, and he was openly critical of Lucic. This actually caused the Sabres to start to question their own team's toughness since not one player on the ice responded immediately when Lucic wiped Miller out. To his credit, center Paul Gaustad had a go at Lucic when the two teams met again in Buffalo, but the damage to the team psyche had already been done. Then, to make matters worse, Gaustad was traded to the Nashville Predators for a first-round pick, which was a move that angered Miller because he thought if the team had any hope of making the postseason, Buffalo needed to retain players like the robust Gaustad.

Needless to say, the Sabres did not qualify for the 2012 playoffs, but if there was any good news to pull from the season, it was that Miller found his old form and nearly pulled his team into the eighth and final playoff spot in the Eastern Conference. As March came to a close, Miller posted a streak of 10–3–2, but it still left the Sabres short of their target and they lost the playoff race to the Washington Capitals by three points, 92 to 89. By the end of the 2011–12 season, however, Miller had played 61 games and won 31 times. He also recorded six shutouts and posted a save percentage of .916 and a goals-against average of 2.55 after absorbing

Buffalo Sabres goalie Ryan Miller has been determined to play the position as early as the age of eight, when he told his father Dean in the middle of a minor hockey game that he wanted to be the goalie. His father, who was coaching the team, had to agree to his son's demands in order to get him back out on the ice, and Miller's on– and off-ice intensity has never waned, as is evident in the way he approaches the NHL.

Miller, however, was a discouraged player for most of the 2011–12 season. The 6-foot-2, 175-pound netminder was made to carry the bulk of the Sabres' hopes, as the club once again continued to be a low-scoring unit. The team's problem with putting pucks in the net has been around for much of Miller's time in Buffalo, but early on in the 2011–12 season, things were par-

1,788 opposition shots. These statistics are near Miller's career marks, but because he had such a poor start to the year, his name was no longer bandied about when considering the best netminders in the NHL in 2011–12.

Nevertheless, the numbers speak for themselves. Since becoming a full-time NHL goalie in 2005–06, Miller has won 30 or more games for the Sabres for seven straight seasons. With him in net, Buffalo has once finished as the best team in the league and has twice appeared in the Eastern Conference championship. Miller was generally acknowledged as the top netminder in the league during the 2009–10 season, and after posting 41 victories, 5 shutouts and a .929 save percentage, he was awarded the Vezina Trophy.

Many hockey fans quite correctly insist that Miller is one of the most valuable players in the entire NHL because his presence between the pipes in Buffalo allows the Sabres to get by on razor-thin goal differentials. Without him, the Sabres don't have much chance of making the playoffs, but it is also widely acknowledged that the team won't get far without an offensive boost, either. Looking ahead to the 2012–13 season, Sabres fans are hoping that Buffalo spends new owner Terry Pegula's money much more wisely and gets Miller the on-ice help he deserves.

Eastern Conference
Team Star

Eric
STAAL
12
CAROLINA HURRICANES – C

were quick to put forward theories that explained what had happened and why.

One explanation suggested that Staal was concerned for his brother Marc, who is a member of the New York Rangers and who was out with a severe concussion that was inflicted by Staal. He tried to downplay how much the injury affected him, but it was clear Staal was not happy he had knocked his own brother out of the lineup. Further proof of this particular theory came when Marc returned to play 46 games during the 2011–12 season, during which time Staal's game picked up significantly.

Another explanation for Carolina's dismal 2011–12 season centers around the coaching change that saw Muller take over behind the bench. It was Muller's first chance at a head-coach position, and after the slow start, the team eventually responded to his leadership. By the time the season was over, Muller posted a 25–20–12 record and Staal was back up to 70 points (24 goals and 46 assists), which was at least one level closer to his usual standard of play. In fact, Staal has recorded 70 or more points for seven consecutive years (his best season saw him record 100 points in 2005–06), but despite his positive end to the season, it was still too late for Carolina to overcome its bad start and make the playoffs. The team's 33–33–16 record had gained them 82 points, which placed them 10 points out of a playoff position.

The question now becomes whether the last portion of the 2011–12 season was a true indicator of where the Hurricanes are headed or if they are still in trouble in the season to come.

History suggests that Staal is simply too good to have another rough start like he did in 2011–12. His résumé alone is enough to suggest that the season was an aberration — Staal was outstanding in the 2006 Stanley Cup playoffs, recording 28 points in 25 postseason games to lead the Hurricanes to the championship; he collected a gold medal wearing a Team Canada uniform

C onsidering that the Carolina Hurricanes' Eric Staal is one of the best players in the NHL, his performance to start the 2011–12 season was, quite frankly, shocking. Normally one of the most productive centers in the game, the 27-year-old Staal scored just one goal in his first 18 games of the season. His slump helped set the stage for the Hurricanes to post an 8–13–4 record that cost head coach Paul Maurice his job. When Maurice was dismissed and replaced by Kirk Muller, Staal was still only at five goals and 11 points and an NHL-worst minus 17. A mere year earlier, Staal was one of the captains at the NHL All-Star Game, but in 2012, he was not even invited to attend. No one had expected such a poor performance from Staal or from the Hurricanes, and pundits and fans alike

at the 2007 World Hockey Championships, chipping in with 10 points in 10 games played; and he won another gold medal with Team Canada at the 2010 Winter Olympics in Vancouver, where he recorded one goal and 6 assists. Further, winning each of hockey's most prestigious championships has put Staal among the select company of the Triple Gold Club.

As Staal enters his prime years, Hurricanes general manager Jim Rutherford addressed the growing concern that his star center would flee the struggling Carolina club by trading for his brother Jordan, a standout forward who had outgrown his role with the Pittsburgh Penguins. The addition of Jordan will give a shot in the arm to the Carolina offense, whose second-highest scorer in 2011–12 behind Eric was Jussi Jokinen, who registered only 46 points.

The brothers' supporting cast of Jeff Skinner, Tuomo Ruutu and Jokinen all have the potential to break out and become more than just role players. And as long as star netminder Cam Ward keeps playing well, the Hurricanes should be an interesting team to watch in upcoming years.

> Drafted 2nd overall by the Carolina Hurricanes in 2003

> Member of Stanley Cup–winning Hurricanes team in 2006

> NHL Second Team All-Star in 2006

> Recorded 70 or more points in seven consecutive seasons

> Recorded 250 goals and 574 points in 642 career games

CAREER HIGHLIGHTS

Stephen WEISS

ebok

FLORIDA PANTHERS – C

9

Panthers lost a tough double overtime Game 7 to the New Jersey Devils, the eventual Eastern Conference champions. Even with the exit, all indications show that the Panthers have great potential.

Weiss played minor hockey in Toronto, Ontario, for the Young Nationals and had 109 points in just 48 games in 1997–98. He played another season in the Toronto area before he went to the Plymouth Whalers of the Ontario Hockey League to start his junior career in 1999–2000. The 5-foot-11, 185-pound Weiss had an excellent first year with the Whalers when he recorded 66 points in 64 games. He added 87 more points in 62 games in 2000–01, his draft year. Weiss was selected fourth overall in the NHL entry draft behind Ilya Kovalchuk, Jason Spezza and Alexander Svitov, and he should have easily gone in Svitov's spot.

As it was, Weiss spent a few years bouncing between the Panthers and their American Hockey League affiliate, playing 77 NHL games in the 2002–03 season. He became a fulltime Panther by the 2006–07 season and he scored 20 goals that year. Weiss slipped back somewhat in 2007–08, but got better when Florida hired coach Peter DeBoer, who also coached him in Plymouth. In 2008–09 Weiss only scored 14 times but had a career high 47 assists and a team leading 61 points along with a plus-19 rating. Weiss was again the team points leader with 60 in 2009–10.

General manager Dale Talon, who was the architect of the Chicago Blackhawks' most recent Stanley Cup win, was hired to run the Florida club in 2010 and has transformed the franchise. Talon made the unpopular but necessary move of unloading talented and tough winger Nathan Horton (as per Horton's request). He also brought in players such as Bryan Campbell, Tomas Fleishmann, Kris Versteeg, Tomas Kopecky and Sean Berengheim to transform the club and allow some of the young talent the Panthers have in development a chance to stay in the American Hockey League, developing in

When Stephen Weiss completed his tenth year as a Florida Panther he set the team record for most seasons with the club — surpassing the nine years each served by Paul Laus and Radek Dvorak. He also set two other team marks during the 2011–12 season: most career games played (637) and most career assists (246). The Toronto native will set more team marks if he stays with the Panthers, and based on his performance in 2011–12 (20 goals, 37 assists), there is no reason to think he won't be a Panther for the foreseeable future. In addition to setting new club records, Weiss also accomplished something much more significant — he helped get the Panthers into the playoffs for the first time in his career. Weiss had 3 goals and 2 assists in the first-round, seven-game series, but the

the minors at a pace better suited to budding NHL prospects. Talon also brought in new coach Kevin Dineen, under whom the Panthers won their first Southeast Division crown.

Weiss was the lone holdover that Talon kept from the previous Panther teams. Dineen relied on Weiss in every situation, including on the power-play and penalty kill. The talented forward continued to perform consistently, collecting 57 points and registering six game-winning goals in 2011–12 to go along with his plus-5 rating. Weiss is working through a six-year contract, and does not want to leave the organization that he believes is going in the right direction.

Time will tell whether Weiss receives his just rewards. In previous campaigns when it came down to the last handful of games in the regular season, when the Panthers were typically out of contention, Weiss found it very difficult to play. Now that he has some NHL playoff experience to draw upon, you can be sure he'll be chomping at the bit to get back into the postseason.

> Drafted 4th overall by the Florida Panthers in 2001

> Scored 20 or more goals four times

> Scored 23 career game-winning goals for the Panthers

> Posted 40 or more points six times

> Recorded 144 goals and 390 points in 637 career games

CAREER HIGHLIGHTS

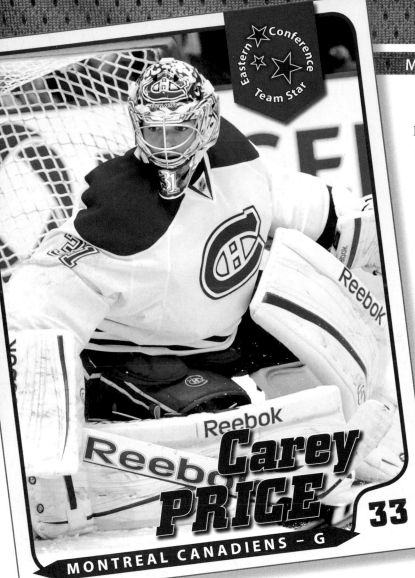

Carey
PRICE

33

MONTREAL CANADIENS – G

Kolzig, who was a part owner of the Americans. By the end of Price's third season with the team, he finished with 24 wins, a 2.34 goals-against average and a .920 save percentage, which earned him enough attention to be drafted fifth overall by the Montreal Canadiens in the 2005 entry draft. He didn't head straight to the Montreal bench, though, and the 6-foot-3, 219-pound Price played two more seasons with Tri-City before being truly recognized as a force to be reckoned with, thanks to his performance on Team Canada at the 2007 World Junior Hockey Championships.

In the semifinals of the tournament in Leksand, Sweden, Canada was facing its archrival, the U.S. The fiercely contested game went to a shootout that included four sudden-death rounds. Price made impressive saves against shots from Patrick Kane and Peter Mueller, and largely because of his final efforts, Canada won the game and moved on to the gold-medal final. The showdown against Russia was never in doubt and the Canadians triumphed 4–2. Price was named the tournament's most valuable player and top goaltender, allowing only seven goals in just six games, and he capped off the year by winning the Del Wilson Trophy (WHL's top goalie) and being named Canadian Hockey League Goaltender of the Year.

Price's good fortune carried through to the spring when he was summoned to the Habs' minor league affiliate, the Hamilton Bulldogs of the American Hockey League, for their playoff run. The Bulldogs, backstopped by Price, won the Calder Cup after completing a five-game series victory over the Hershey Bears. Accepting more accolades, Price took home the Jack A. Butterfield Trophy as playoff MVP, posting a record of 15–6, with two shutouts and a .936 save percentage.

When Price made the NHL's 2007–08 All-Rookie Team in his debut year with the Canadiens (in which he also posted a 24–12–3 record in 41 games played), his future in Montreal appeared to be cemented. The team even named him as their starting netminder by trading

C arey Price's meteoric rise to stardom seemed almost too good to be true, but after five up and down seasons, the Anahim Lake, British Columbia, native has officially asserted himself as a bona fide NHL goalie.

Price's father, Jerry, was drafted by the Philadelphia Flyers in 1978, and while he never did crack an NHL lineup, his turn in the minor-pro ranks was undoubtedly instrumental in Price's development. Father and son traveled together, constantly moving to larger communities with higher caliber hockey, and by the 2002–03 season, Price found himself playing junior hockey for the Tri-City Americans of the Western Hockey League (WHL). He was a stellar performer and had the good fortune to train under former NHL netminder Olif

away veteran Cristobal Huet to the Washington Capitals. Price, however, faced adversity in 2008–09 in a sophomore year that was riddled with injury and inconsistency. He found himself competing for ice time with backup goalie Jaroslav Halak, and while Price was named as the starter for Montreal's Eastern Conference quarterfinal against the Boston Bruins, the Canadiens were dispatched in a four-game sweep. In 2009–10, Price was relegated to the bench as Halak unexpectedly led Montreal to the semifinals in a run that included seventh-game upset victories over both Washington and the Pittsburgh Penguins. Yet, despite Halak's goaltending success, the Habs dealt him in the off-season to the St. Louis Blues.

Price responded to the criticism with a stellar campaign in 2010–11. He finished the season tied for wins (38) with Roberto Luongo and his durability was on display as he finished second overall in minutes played (4,206) and games played (72). In the playoffs, however, the Canadiens lost Game 7 of their first-round playoff series to their nemesis, the Boston Bruins.

The 2011–12 season remained tumultuous for the team, as it went through changes to players, coaches and managers. Nevertheless, Price weathered the storm,

posting a 2.43 goals-against average and a 9.16 save percentage. But, even Price couldn't escape completely unscathed, and he suffered a season-ending concussion in April 2012.

Price, however, has largely managed to overcome the tribulations that come with the territory of playing in the rabid Montreal market. His signing of a six-year, $39 million contract extension on July 2nd, 2012 shows that new general manager Marc Bergevin, and the rest of the Montreal brain trust have zero doubts that Price is the man for them.

> Drafted 5th overall by the Montreal Canadiens in 2005

> Named to the NHL All-Rookie Team in 2008

> Recorded 23 or more wins in a season four times

> Led the league in wins with 38 in 2010–11

> Posted a 124–104–35 record in 271 career games

CAREER HIGHLIGHTS

Eastern Conference Team Star

John TAVARES 91
NEW YORK ISLANDERS – C

Tavares has been a special hockey player since he started out on the ice when he was six years old. It was at this age that he was already able to lift the puck off the ice, and it was therefore no wonder that he was the best and most talented player wherever he went. One of the most prominent role models in Tavares' life was his uncle, John, who was an outstanding lacrosse player. Tavares admired his uncle's work ethic and passion for his favorite sport, and he loved to stay close to the lacrosse action as a ball boy when the Buffalo Bandits played their games.

By the age of 15, Tavares was deemed to be an exceptional player and was allowed to join the Oshawa Generals of the Ontario Hockey League (OHL) one year early. He played in four OHL seasons and recorded an astounding 433 points (215 goals and 218 assists) in just 247 games. By the time his junior career was over, Tavares was pretty much the consensus best player available for the 2009 draft. He also had two World Junior Championship titles to his name and he still cherishes the memories of those two back-to-back victories in 2008 and 2009 while he was playing for Team Canada. After being drafted by the Islanders, the hope was that Tavares would be the main building block to the start of a new era for a floundering team that had once enjoyed greatness.

Tavares has done a pretty good job of living up to his advanced billing. His rookie season saw him score 24 times (and total 54 points), and he seemed to specialize on the power play since 11 of his goals came with the extra man. He was also named to the NHL's All-Rookie Team and came back with a solid second season that saw him score 29 times and get his point total up to 67. Tavares excelled even more in his third NHL season, but the Islanders have still not made the playoffs (they finished 14th overall in the Eastern Conference after the 2011–12 season), and the hopes of making the postseason are not looking good for the immediate future.

If there was one thing New York Islanders center John Tavares had to improve, it was his skating. He could do everything else superbly, but his skating was holding him back from being a truly elite player. Fortunately, Tavares was never one to back away from a challenge and he was willing to work at his deficiencies during the 2011–12 season, where his hard work paid off. It was noticeable that the 6-foot, 202-pound Tavares was faster on his blades and more succinct in his movements, and his newfound skills resulted in his best year in the NHL with 31 goals and 81 points (which were both career highs). And, now that Tavares is achieving at superstar levels, it would be great if the entire Islanders team would join him in reaching new heights.

The Islanders have had a hard time attracting top-notch talent to play alongside Tavares. Players like Matt Moulson (36 goals in 2011–12) and P.A. Parenteau (67 points in 2011–12) preformed well with Tavares in the past, but with Parenteau's departure and the signing of Brad Boyes, the Islanders are still without high-end performers to help out the slick-scoring center. Unless Islanders management starts to surround Tavares with better talent, the skilled youngster will likely be watching the playoffs on TV for a few more years. Tavares, too, has his own work to do: he is committed to the New York team until the 2017–18 season, and he needs to show that he can be an Islanders star in the mold of Bryan Trottier or Mike Bossy and carry on to lead his team back to glory.

> Drafted 1st overall by the New York Islanders in 2009
> Named to the NHL's All-Rookie Team In 2010
> Scored 24 or more goals in each of his first three NHL seasons
> Scored a career-high 31 times in 2011–12
> Recorded 84 goals and 202 points in 243 career games

CAREER HIGHLIGHTS

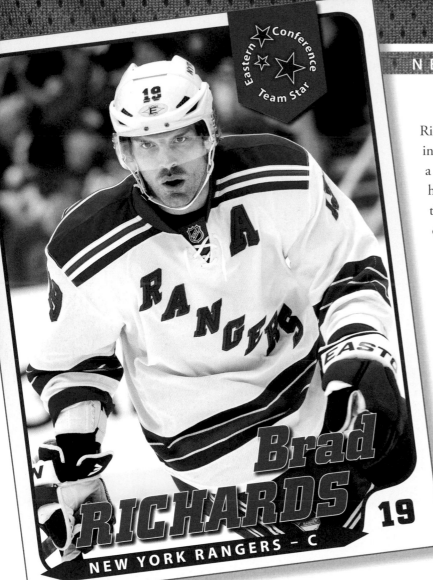

Brad
RICHARDS
NEW YORK RANGERS – C
19

Richards' results were under-achieving at first, both individually and in terms of team play. Richards has a flair for the dramatic and for being a clutch player; he eventually demonstrated that for the Rangers in the regular season and most importantly in the play-offs. With each passing game Richards' performance improved, to the point where he finished with 25 goals and 41 assists, good enough for 66 points and second on team scoring behind Marian Gaborik (who had 76 points during the 2011–12 season). Richards ended up tied for the most game-winning goals (along with team captain Ryan Callahan) with nine, and he potted seven goals with the extra man.

Part of the reason why Richards struggled early on was that Tortorella used a different coaching approach with the Rangers than with the Lightning, the team on which they had previously established a relationship. As boss of the New York bench Tortorella made it clear the team was going to play a hard-edged defensive game where it was expected that checking and blocking shots was just as valued as scoring goals. Two-way hockey was the way the Rangers were going to win playing in front of all-world goalie Henrik Lundqvist. It took a while for Richards to adapt, but he learned to be effective while adhering to the new coaching style. It all worked out well for the Rangers club, which finished first overall in the Eastern Conference during the regular season.

Richards was always seen as a key playoff performer and the 2012 playoffs helped to solidify his reputation. The primetime center only scored six goals, but those he scored were big. The first came against Ottawa in the sixth game of the series with the Rangers facing elimination. First, he helped set up the opening goal for his team, and then he scored a power-play marker to give New York the lead in a game they would win by a 3–2 score. The Rangers then won the seventh game at home before facing the Washington Capitals in the next series. During the fifth game of the Capitals series, Richards

When the NHL free agency period begins every summer, there tends to be a feeding frenzy around the best players available. When the day came in 2011 there was really only one major unrestricted player to be signed — center Brad Richards who had enjoyed a stellar career with the Tampa Bay Lightning and the Dallas Stars. Richards was courted by many teams. Yet in the end he knew exactly where he wanted to be, with his former Tampa Bay coach John Tortorella, playing for the New York Rangers. On July 2, 2011 Richards signed a contract worth $60 million over nine seasons.

Large contracts like the one Richards signed with the Rangers bring about high expectations, and slow starts are not tolerated very well by a demanding fan base.

scored a goal with just eight seconds to play, tying the game 2–2 and sending it to overtime. New York scored in the extra session to gain the series lead and eventually took out the Washington side in seven games. Naturally it was Richards who scored the opening goal in the final game versus the Capitals.

However the New Jersey Devils kept Richards from scoring any goals in the Eastern Conference final and the Rangers lost in six games, dashing any hopes for their first Stanley Cup since 1994. The slick pivot needs help on the attack if he is to lead the Rangers back to the Cup final. Having newly acquired right-winger Rick Nash on his line will no doubt help Richards in showcasing his superb playmaking skills. It goes to show, no matter how good one player is, hockey is still very much a team game.

> Drafted 64th overall by the Tampa Bay Lightning in 1998

> Named winner of the Conn Smythe Trophy in 2004

> Named winner of the Lady Byng Memorial Trophy in 2004

> Twice recorded 91-point seasons

> Recorded 245 goals and 782 points in 854 career games

CAREER HIGHLIGHTS

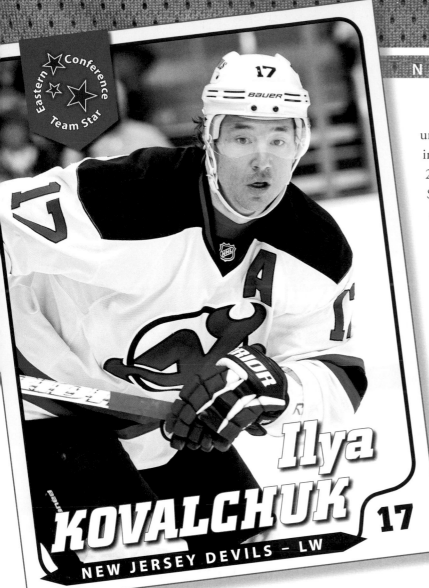

Eastern Conference Team Star

Ilya
KOVALCHUK 17
NEW JERSEY DEVILS – LW

unfortunately, was a year that saw the Devils ousted in the first round of the playoffs. The next season in 2010–11 saw Kovalchuk sign a monster deal worth $100 million over 15 seasons, but it was no secret he didn't like head coach John MacLean. It was only at the end of the year, when the Devils replaced MacLean with Jacques Lemaire to finish off the 2010–11 campaign, that Kovalchuk felt respected and utilized properly.

The 2011–12 season represented a new start for Kovalchuk under head coach Peter DeBoer. The flashy winger was given more responsibility and ice time by the new bench boss, and he responded with a 37-goal season while totaling 83 points, which put him in fifth place among all NHL scorers. The return of Zach Parise (who scored 31 times in 2011–12) to the Devils' lineup was also a big help because he was able to take some of the pressure off Kovalchuk's shoulders. And so, in addition to leading the Devils in goals and points in 2011–12, Kovalchuk scored seven game-deciding goals in shootouts, which helped the Devils earn seven very valuable points in the tight Eastern Conference playoff race.

Kovalchuk uses all of his physical gifts to be a feared player. He has a tremendous, high-powered shot that he can unleash on the net with deadly accuracy, and while goalies know it's coming, most of the time they are helpless to make the stop, which is why Kovalchuk has scored 406 goals through the end of the 2011–12 season. He is also an excellent skater who knows when to turn on the jets to get in the clear, and he is quite willing to use his large frame to protect the puck. Further, he can make precise passes to open teammates (he has recorded over 40 assists in a season five times thus far), but sometimes over-passes the puck when he should be firing it on the net. He is, however, getting better defensively.

The 2012 playoffs were another sort of reawakening for Kovalchuk, who helped take the sixth-seeded Devils

It might sound strange, but since Ilya Kovalchuk has become a New Jersey Devil, he has scored less often yet has become a better hockey player. The 6-foot-3, 230-pound winger has bought into the Devil's style of play, which likely means any chance at a 50-goal season is a thing of the past for the talented Kovalchuk. A 40-goal season might be realistic, but the Russian-born Kovalchuk seems to thrive more on a club that emphasizes a team game rather than one built around individual talents. In fact, it was not an easy transition for Kovalchuk when he first arrived in New Jersey because he was used to being the go-to guy for the Atlanta Thrashers (the team that drafted him first overall in 2001). The Devils actually gave up three players to acquire Kovalchuk late in the 2009–10 season, but this,

all the way to the Stanley Cup final. He was at his best in the second round when the New Jersey side pulled off a six-game series triumph over the Philadelphia Flyers. Kovalchuk recorded seven points versus Philadelphia and had 19 points in 23 postseason games. He faltered badly, however, in the final versus the Los Angeles Kings when it was obvious he was not able to play at full speed. The Kings, in fact, did a masterful job of checking Kovalchuk and Parise and were thus able to walk away with the championship.

The Devils have slowly rebuilt their team over the last number of years, but Kovalchuk still remains a cornerstone, especially with the departure of Parise during the 2012 offseason. The question now will be: Has he taken up too much money to allow the Devils to keep other key components on the team or to add new ones in the future? If he can keep the Devils in contention for most

of the time he has left on his deal, many will consider the high cost of re-signing him (plus a restructuring of his contract) a worthwhile investment.

- Drafted 1st overall by the Atlanta Thrashers in 2001
- Scored 41 or more goals six times
- Two-time 50+ goal-scorer with the Thrashers
- Two-time NHL First Team All–Star
- Recorded 406 goals and 785 points in 779 career games

CAREER HIGHLIGHTS

Eastern Conference Team Star

Jason **SPEZZA** 19

OTTAWA SENATORS – C

been a top point producer. After starting out at 14 years old with the Toronto Marlboros in 1997–98, Spezza achieved 114 points in just 54 games. Four years later, he recorded a 116-point season while playing with two Ontario Hockey League teams before he was traded to the Belleville Bulls, where he finished his junior eligibility. His path to the NHL seemed clear.

When Ottawa traded star center Alexei Yashin to the New York Islanders, they received defenseman Zdeno Chara and a first-round draft pick in return. That draft pick turned out to be Spezza, and he made an already lopsided deal even better. Spezza, however, had a lot to learn and coach Jacques Martin said he was not ready to play in the NHL. Spezza was hurt at being sent down, but two years with the American Hockey League's (AHL's) Binghamton Senators did Spezza a world of good. In 2004–05, when the NHL players were locked out, it was Spezza who lead the AHL in points with 117 (32 goals and 85 assists), which gave him the confidence to play at the NHL level.

After a 90-point season in 2005–06, Spezza scored 34 goals and added 53 assists during the 2006–07 regular season. Additionally, the 2007 playoffs saw Ottawa go all the way to the Stanley Cup final, even though they were soundly beaten by the Anaheim Ducks in five games. For all intents and purposes, it looked like the talented center had arrived, but he continued to be a target for the fans and the media as his game continued to be streaky and his off-ice actions rang of immaturity.

Spezza appreciated the passion of the fans, but he hasn't necessarily understood or agreed with his critics. He always has a grin on his face and seems to smile no matter what the situation, and some have always taken his happy-go-lucky style the wrong way. It has driven many of his coaches to frustration, but Spezza's talent level is too great to stay angry at him for long. Besides, there is no way Spezza's coaches can ever change his game too radically because there are simply so few players with his skill set at center.

Everyone noticed that the Ottawa Senators' star center Jason Spezza was somehow different during the 2011–12 season, and, indeed, a more mature approach to life both on and off the ice made for a new man and player. In uniform, Spezza was by far the best player on the surprising Senators team that snagged a playoff position when it was supposed to be one of the worst squads in the league according to preseason predictions. The rejuvenated Spezza had one of his best years yet with 34 goals and 84 points, which placed him fourth in league scoring. He was also more of a leader than ever before, and he seemed to take his position as assistant captain much more seriously after longtime Senators Chris Kelly and Mike Fisher were traded.

Spezza, a native of Mississauga, Ontario, has always

There's no denying, however, that the 6-foot-3, 216-pound Spezza has matured into a seasoned player. He is now defensively much more responsible (he was plus 11 in 2011–12) and he does not try to make the most difficult play every time he's on the ice. Spezza's hands are still soft and his blazing shot is evident, but he has learned to use his teammates more effectively in all situations. He is also still deadly on the power play, scoring 10 goals with the extra man in 2011–12.

For Spezza, the next five years will be telling. Daniel Alfredsson is likely going to retire soon, which will place Spezza in a prime position to become team captain. If he gets the coveted "C," it will complete quite the turnaround for one of the most talented players in the league.

> Drafted 2nd overall by the Ottawa Senators in 2001
> Recorded 390 career assists
> Scored 34 goals in a season three times
> Recorded 70 or more points five times
> Recorded 226 goals and 616 points in 606 career games

CAREER HIGHLIGHTS

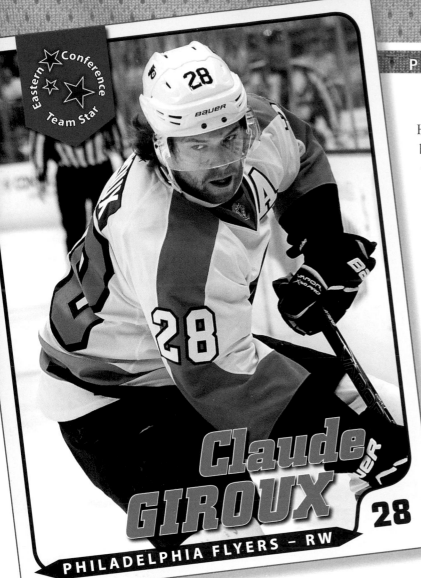

Claude
GIROUX
28
PHILADELPHIA FLYERS – RW

Hockey League, it looked as if their worst fears might be realized. Giroux, however, did not give up, and when he was 17 years old, he played for the Cumberland Grads (in the Canadian Junior Hockey League) for the 2004–05 season. He produced a respectable 40 points in 48 games, and someone with a sharp hockey sense later suggested to the coach of the Gatineau Olympiques [in the Quebec Major Junior Hockey League (QMJHL)] that he take a look at Giroux.

Giroux did not overwhelm Gatineau coach Benoit Groulx, but whatever he did was enough because Groulx invited Giroux to training camp for the start of the next season. It was there that he wowed the Olympiques' coaching staff, which earned him three seasons in the Quebec town just across the river from Ottawa.

Giroux never recorded less than 103 points in any season with the Olympiques, and his impressive play in the QMJHL (321 points in just 187 games) caught the eye of pro scouts. Under the impression that either the Montreal Canadiens (his favorite team growing up) or the New York Rangers were going to take him with the 20th or 21st pick of the 2006 NHL entry draft, Giroux found out he was sorely mistaken when both teams passed on selecting him. In the end, the Philadelphia Flyers took him with the 22nd selection because Philadelphia scout, Simon Nolet, and the team's director of hockey operations, Chris Pryor, liked Giroux's temperament and his tremendous skill level. True, Philadelphia legend Bobby Clarke forgot Giroux's name when he went to the podium to make the selection for the Flyers, but it was in very short order that everyone knew who the 5-foot-11, 172-pound Giroux was and why he was selected in the first round.

To start, the Flyers let Giroux go back to junior hockey where he had a great year in 2007–08, winning a gold medal with Team Canada at the World Juniors and taking the Quebec league championship with the Olympiques, a series in which he recorded 51 points in

C laude Giroux started playing hockey in the small town of Hearst, Ontario, where he lived with his family and dreamed of playing in the NHL. So, as his skill level began to outgrow the minor hockey available in his hometown, Giroux's family had a decision to make: leave Hearst so Giroux could play hockey in a bigger market that would better accommodate his skills, or stay put and hope for the best. In the end, with their son's best interests at heart, the Girouxs moved their family to Ottawa, Ontario.

It was never a sure thing that Giroux was going to make it in hockey, and while his family was under no illusion about his chances, they wanted, at the very least, to have him exposed to the best opportunities possible. And then, when Giroux went undrafted in the Ontario

just 19 playoff games. Afterward, he turned pro with the Flyers' farm team, the Philadelphia Phantoms of the American Hockey League, and had 34 points in 33 games before getting called up to the big club for the final 42 games of the 2008–09 season.

Since then, Giroux has recorded 243 points in 287 regular-season games as a Flyer, and the 2011–12 campaign saw him finish third in league scoring with 93 points (28 goals and 65 assists). He was especially good in the 2012 playoffs, as he achieved 17 points in only 10 games and led his team past Sidney Crosby and the Pittsburgh Penguins in the opening round before being ousted from competition by the New Jersey Devils.

Aside from his ability to score points, Giroux has developed a feisty approach that makes him not only one of the grittiest players in the NHL, but also one of the league's top players. Some in the hockey know have even said — Giroux's own coach Peter Laviolette included — that he is the

best player in the world. Such praise is pretty heady, but the fact is that Giroux's name is in conversations of this caliber and if he continues to play consistently (like he did in 2011–12), a future claim to the same effect might be met with nods all around.

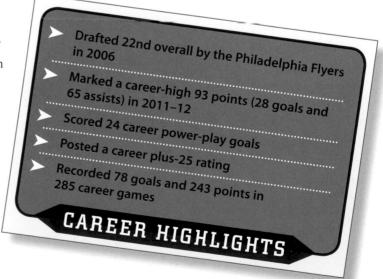

➤ Drafted 22nd overall by the Philadelphia Flyers in 2006

➤ Marked a career-high 93 points (28 goals and 65 assists) in 2011–12

➤ Scored 24 career power-play goals

➤ Posted a career plus-25 rating

➤ Recorded 78 goals and 243 points in 285 career games

CAREER HIGHLIGHTS

Eastern Conference Team Star

Sidney CROSBY 87

PITTSBURGH PENGUINS – C

U p until the 2010–11 season, everything was going well for Sidney Crosby. He was drafted by the Pittsburgh Penguins with the first overall selection in the 2005 draft, and he was named the team's captain, as well as a First Team All-Star and the NHL's most valuable player; he has twice recorded over 100 points in a season and has once produced a 51-goal season and been the league's leading goal scorer. He also won the 2009 Stanley Cup and added a gold medal to his résumé while playing for Team Canada at the 2010 Olympics. In short, Crosby had done it all by the ripe old age of 22 and it looked like the best was yet to come. Then, during the 2010-11 season, as he was leading the league in scoring (with 66 points after just 40 games), everything came to a crashing halt after one

devastating blow to the head and a hit from behind into the boards.

On a rainy night on January 1, 2011, when the Penguins were playing the Washington Capitals in the outdoor Winter Classic, Crosby was hit on his blind side (some say inadvertently) by 6-foot-5, 220-pound Washington forward David Steckel. Crosby took the full force of the hit and briefly lay stunned on the ice. He was, however, able to get up and return to the Pittsburgh bench; he even played in the final period of the game. Crosby also played in the Penguins' next game, and in that tilt against the Tampa Bay Lightning, he was crunched into the boards behind the net by Lightning defenseman Victor Hedman. The two hits spelled the end of Crosby's season and any hopes for a scoring title or the chance to take home another championship.

The recovery time Crosby needed for his concussion led to unsubstantiated talk about his retirement, and the media had a field day with their speculations. A press conference in the summer of 2011 — with only doctors present — served to add fuel to the fire, but the fact of that matter was that Crosby only wanted privacy in which to deal with his injuries. In the end, none of it mattered, as he was unable to start the 2011–12 season.

Finally, though, after much anticipation, Crosby was ready. He took to the ice against the New York Islanders at home on November 21, 2011, and in typical Crosby style, it was a memorable game. The Penguins easily won 5–0 with Crosby tallying two goals and two assists while earning the first-star-of-the-game honors. The Pittsburgh crowd raucously chanted his name and everyone, including the kid from Cole Harbour, Nova Scotia, went home happy.

Then the unthinkable happened. On December 5, 2011, when the visiting Boston Bruins beat the Penguins 3–1, Crosby suffered another concussion. This time he was out until the middle of March 2012 and there were those who were questioning just how resilient

Crosby was. The 5-foot-11, 200-pound center, however, ignored the pressure and did the right thing by taking the time to recover properly. He consulted other doctors and found that a neck injury, overlooked from his first concussion, might have been the root of his problems all along. Crosby's efforts at rehabilitation did little to silence his naysayers. Analyst Mike Milbury and New York Rangers coach John Tortorella were especially critical of the Pittsburgh captain, but in the end Crosby did what was best and wound up playing 22 games and posting 37 points (8 goals and 29 assists) in the 2011–12 season.

Later, in the playoffs, the Philadelphia Flyers were able to outscore the Penguins and eliminate them in six games during the first round. Crosby had three goals and five points, but his playoffs were more memorable for the emotions he displayed. The fiercely competitive centerman who is normally calm and reserved was uncharacteristically petulant and undisciplined. His raw reactions were pure "Sid the Kid" — all in and all heart.

Again, the critics piled on top of him, but after Crosby's frustrating road to recovery, his lack of discipline should have been forgiven. The expectation now, however, is that when Crosby and the Penguins return to action in 2012–13, the captain will be in top form — both physically and mentally — and will be ready to lead Pittsburgh back to the promised land.

- Drafted 1st overall by the Pittsburgh Penguins in 2005
- Named winner of the Hart Memorial Trophy in 2007
- Led the NHL in goals scored with 51 in 2009–10
- Two-time NHL First Team All-Star
- Recorded 223 goals and 609 points in 434 career games

CAREER HIGHLIGHTS

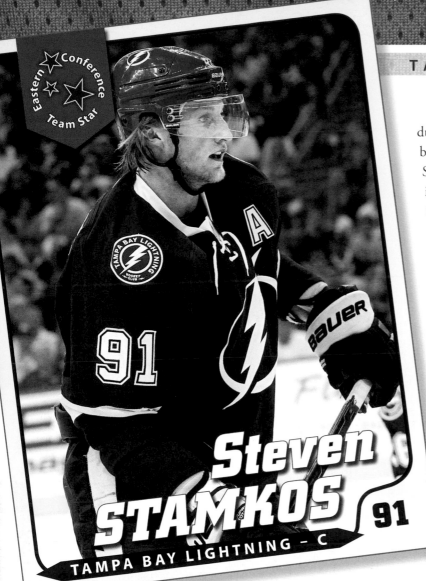

Eastern Conference
Team Star

Steven STAMKOS 91
TAMPA BAY LIGHTNING – C

during the early part of a rookie year is a hard way to break into the league. Fortunately, the 18-year-old Stamkos showed resilience, scoring 23 goals and totaling 46 points in his first year in the NHL — a most impressive performance.

Just one year later, in 2009–10, Stamkos shared the league lead with Sidney Crosby in goals scored, with 51. Stamkos was simply outstanding on the power play, with 24 goals and a 95-point total that ranked him fifth overall. It was also during this season that fans saw Stamkos unleash his vaunted one-timer, which is a play he usually likes to use when his team has the 5-on-4 advantage. What Stamkos does is station himself near the top of the faceoff circle before blasting away when he takes a cross-ice pass. In subsequent seasons opposing teams started to pay more attention to Stamkos when the Lightning had the extra man, but he still managed 17 power-play goals in the 2010–11 campaign. His 91 points that season also helped the Lightning get back into the playoffs, and they nearly made it to the Stanley Cup finals after coming up just one game short.

One of Stamkos' biggest attributes is his constant desire to improve in all aspects of the game, and while he still unleashes his one-timer, he does not hesitate to get in front of the net to tip in a shot or make a drive to the net in search of rebounds. He scored a league-best 60 goals in 2010–11 (10 more than second-place Malkin) and shattered the Lightning team record that was previously held by Lecavalier, who had 52 goals in 2006–07.

By the end of the 2011–12 season, fans all over the NHL were watching on a nightly basis to see if Stamkos was going to once again hit the 60 mark. A late-season visit to Ontario to play against the Toronto Maple Leafs even saw Leafs Nation cheering on Stamkos, who had 58 goals going into the game. He scored his 59th that night and he potted No. 60 versus the Winnipeg Jets two days later.

While Sidney Crosby suffered from concussion issues over the past two seasons, many experts wondered if the NHL had another player who could step up and become "the face of the game." The search for a marquee player went in different directions. Should it be Alex Ovechkin? Evgeni Malkin? Jonathan Toews? What about a rising star like Taylor Hall? Each was a player worthy of consideration, but there was one standout who at first flew under the radar to capture the unofficial title: Steven Stamkos.

It's true that Stamkos got off to a rocky start after going first overall to the Tampa Bay Lightning in the 2008 entry draft, but the Lightning have never handled their young stars very well (Vincent Lecavalier being the best example), and having a coach like Barry Melrose

Stamkos' performance in 2011–12 (which also featured a career-best 97 points and a team-record 12 game-winning tallies) was actually quite remarkable since the Tampa Bay club tends to worry about defense first under coach Guy Boucher. Part of Stamkos' success is likely due to his line pairing with wily veteran Martin St. Louis, who himself ended up with 74 points at the somewhat advanced age of 36.

The Tampa Bay squad is managed by Steve Yzerman, a Hall of Fame player who should understand exactly what Stamkos is going through as a rising star in the NHL. It's likely Yzerman appreciates what he has in Stamkos and knows he must do everything possible to build a team around his most talented player. Stamkos also seems to have the right personality for the job because few — if any — negative words are ever uttered about the ever-accommodating centerman.

Stamkos was never the biggest or the strongest player on the ice, but the chiseled 6-foot-1, 188-pound center has kept himself in excellent shape, and he is ready to lead his team into the future as the new face of the NHL.

- ▶ Drafted 1st overall by the Tampa Bay Lightning in 2008
- ▶ Two-time winner of the Maurice Richard Trophy
- ▶ Two-time NHL Second Team All-Star
- ▶ Recorded over 90 points in each of the last three seasons
- ▶ Recorded 179 goals and 329 points in 325 career games

CAREER HIGHLIGHTS

Eastern Conference Team Star

Phil **KESSEL** 81
TORONTO MAPLE LEAFS – C

Kessel has been under constant scrutiny ever since joining the Maple Leafs for the 2009–10 season, after a deal was completed with the Boston Bruins. The Leafs, under the direction of general manager Brian Burke, decided to pay a high price for Kessel, conceding three high draft choices (including two in the first round, one of whom was young sensation Tyler Seguin). Kessel, however, has never complained about the badgering he has received from the Toronto media over comparisons as to which team "won" the deal. But, at the same time, he also does not relish standing in front of cameras or speaking with reporters. Quiet, reserved and downright shy, Kessel usually only speaks when he has to. Teammates explain Kessel as a simple guy who likes golf and fishing, and as someone who is considered a good influence in the locker room.

On the ice, it's a completely different story. Kessel lets his natural talent do all the talking, and it speaks loudly and clearly. Kessel is an extremely fast player and his speed gives him the opportunity to take the puck wide on any defenseman in the league. He is also a deft puckhandler who can shoot in stride and in mid-deke, and he can do so through on-ice traffic where his laser of a snap shot is particularly dangerous. Kessel has already scored 165 goals in just six seasons, and he completed his best season in 2011–12 when he had 37 goals and 45 assists for 82 points, which were totals that displayed Kessel as a predominant goal-scorer but also as a playmaker.

Despite Kessel's excellent year, which included a trip to the 2012 All-Star Game (where he was spared last pick), he was still the target of some deserved criticism. Kessel was a plus player for most of the year, but he ended up a minus 10 on the season. Part of that poor record was because of the fact that he lost linemate Joffrey Lupul in early March, after the two players had enjoyed marvellous on-ice chemistry. The other half of the problem was that Kessel didn't work hard enough along the boards in his own end, where he lost battles

When the National Hockey League debuted its new school-yard team-selection system for the 2011 All-Star Game, it was Toronto Maple Leafs right-winger Phil Kessel who was left high and dry. Team captains took turns selecting players until it came down to the final two, and it was Kessel who sat alone waiting for someone to call out his name. Nicklas Lidstrom finally selected him and the humiliation was over with. Kessel seemed to take it all in good humor, but it had to hurt a little, especially after having proven himself to be an elite NHL goal scorer (in 2010–11 he posted his third consecutive 30-goal season, finishing with 32). However, when you beat cancer in your 20s — as Kessel has — perhaps something like being picked last is too trivial to get upset about.

and 50-50 pucks. He also gave the puck away too often while on the rush.

If the Maple Leafs are to improve and have a hope of making the playoffs, Kessel will have to amp up his game. A 40-plus goal season is not out of the question for the lightning-quick winger, and his case would be helped if the Toronto club would secure a legitimate first-line NHL center for Kessel to play with. This has been a point of contention for fans since Kessel arrived in Toronto, and as the club's franchise player, the Leafs and fans alike will continually expect more out of him. Whether this is fair or not, the simple fact of the matter is that it will be on Kessel's shoulders if Toronto succeeds or fails in 2012–13.

- ➤ Drafted 5th overall by the Boston Bruins in 2006
- ➤ Scored 30 or more goals in four straight seasons
- ➤ Recorded a career high in points with 82 (37 goals and 45 assists) in 2011–12
- ➤ Scored 10 power-play goals in 2011–12
- ➤ Recorded 165 goals and 327 points in 456 career games

CAREER HIGHLIGHTS

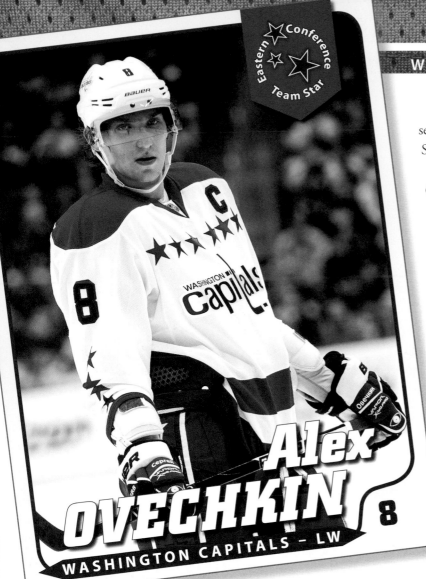

Alex OVECHKIN

WASHINGTON CAPITALS – LW

Eastern Conference Team Star

seem to matter. "Ovie" would always save the day. Sadly, those memorable moments all seem in the past.

Drafted first overall by the Capitals in 2004, the 6-foot-2, 233-pound winger's first five seasons saw him net at least 46 goals and as many as 65. He was a league All-Star every year and won the most prestigious of the major awards, including the Calder Memorial Trophy, the Hart Memorial Trophy (twice), the Art Ross Trophy and the Maurice Richard Trophy (twice). He recorded over 100 points in four of his first five seasons and was the undisputed leader of the Washington club.

It was at the 2010 Winter Olympics in Vancouver that Ovechkin's play began to be less than stellar. His Russian team went out of the tournament early and the expected showdown between Ovechkin and Sidney Crosby of Team Canada failed to materialize. Crosby eventually scored the golden goal for Canada, winning the Olympic gold medal. It could have been a defining moment for Ovechkin, but it did not go his way.

When Bruce Boudreau took over the coaching reins of the Capitals in 2007, it looked like he was the right man to direct the talented Russian. And the duo did click — for a while. Boudreau appreciated Ovechkin's skill set and wanted to unleash his star each and every night on the opposition, who often had difficulty containing the highly charged winger.

However, in the 2009–10 playoffs, when it mattered most, the Montreal Canadiens found a way to contain Ovechkin on the way to beating Washington in seven games. Despite his recording 10 points in the series, the Canadiens effectively shut Ovechkin down in the final contest (a 2–1 win by the Habs). Then in the 2011 postseason the Capitals were ousted in four games by the Tampa Bay Lightning during the second round and more questions were being asked of the Washington star.

Ovechkin argued with Boudreau during a late game time-out early in the 2011–12 season. It was not a good sign. The Capitals quickly turned to former player Dale

What happened to Alex Ovechkin? The Russian sniper who performed at a superstar level from the moment he joined the Washington Capitals in the 2005–06 season disappeared. His production started to slow during the 2010–11 season, and for almost all of the 2011–12 campaign the former superstar became merely ordinary, finishing with 38 goals and 65 points in 78 games.

True, most players would be lucky to play that well, but ordinary is not what hockey fans have come to expect from the sublime left-winger. Ovechkin's combination of size, speed and skill made the Capitals a true contender — not to mention one of the NHL's glamor teams — as he scored one highlight reel goal after the other. Most of his teammates couldn't keep up with him, but it didn't

Hunter to replace Boudreau as coach. Hunter implemented a very different style of play for the Washington team, focusing more on defensive responsibility and shot blocking. Making matters even more difficult, top center Nicklas Backstrom, who Ovechkin had a great on-ice rapport with, was absent for 40 games that season.

The Capitals managed to grind out a 107-point season, but Ovechkin's ice time was reduced by nearly

two minutes per game. It may sound like a small number, but to a thoroughbred like Ovechkin two minutes makes a world of difference. In the playoffs the Capitals rode top goaltending by Braden Holtby to a first-round win and major upset over the Boston Bruins. They nearly edged out the New York Rangers, too, but a close Game 7 loss ended the season. Ovechkin tried to be the best team player possible by back-checking and blocking shots, and he managed to score five goals and four assists in 14 playoff games, but it seemed like a struggle for the talented player.

Hunter returned to coach junior hockey after the 2011–12 season, and the Capitals have hired Hockey Hall of Famer and former Capitals player Adam Oates as his replacement. Here's hoping that Oates can find a middle ground with Ovechkin that sees him playing a more defensively responsible game while still tearing it up offensively. If that happens, it will be up to Ovechkin to show the NHL a few new tricks on the way to regaining his old form.

CAREER HIGHLIGHTS

➤ Drafted 1st overall by the Washington Capitals in 2004

➤ Five-time NHL First Team All-Star

➤ Two-time winner of the Hart Memorial Trophy

➤ Winner of the Art Ross Trophy for the 2007–08 season

➤ Recorded 339 goals and 679 points in 553 career games

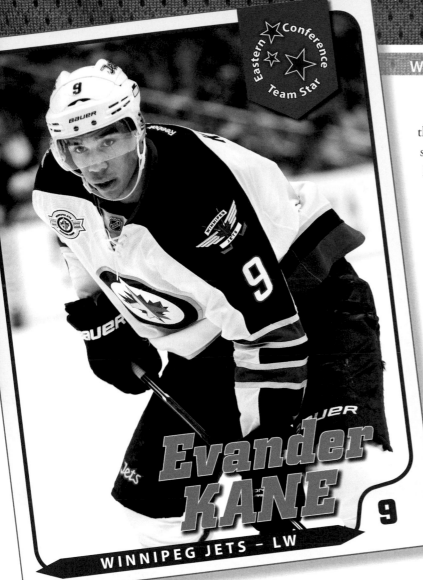

Eastern Conference Team Star

Evander KANE

WINNIPEG JETS – LW

9

the 2011–12 campaign (Kane's third in the NHL), he scored 30 goals, and it was a glimpse of what many have come to expect of the young star.

Kane was born and raised in Vancouver, British Columbia, and was a good all-round athlete who excelled in hockey, basketball, baseball and soccer. He was especially good at hockey, though, and notched 140 points in just 66 games when he played bantam hockey for the North Shore Winter Club. Kane also played for the Greater Vancouver Canadians of the British Columbia Major Midget League and had 22 goals and 54 points in 30 games. In 2006, he was drafted by his hometown Vancouver Giants of the Western Hockey League, and as a 15 year old he played in two games at the 2007 Memorial Cup tournament, which the Giants won. Following this, in 2007–08, his first full year of junior play, Kane scored 24 goals. In his second season, his total jumped to 48, and that year he was made a member of Team Canada at the World Junior Championships. Granted, he made his way onto the club as an injury reserve and as the youngest player on the team, but he ended up showcasing his talent by collecting six points in six games.

Leading up to the 2009 NHL entry draft, most of the pre-draft attention was going to John Tavares, Victor Hedman and Matt Duchene, who were selected, respectively, first, second and third. Kane was chosen fourth overall by the Atlanta Thrashers, and he just might turn out to be the most effective player of the group. Kane's selection, however, also held a different significance — it marked the highest a black player has ever been chosen by an NHL team.

Kane made the Atlanta lineup to start the 2009–10 season and recorded an assist in his first game. One game later, he scored his first career goal (the game-winner) against the St. Louis Blues in a 3–2 Atlanta victory. Overall, Kane had a bit of an up-and-down year, but he still managed to score 14 goals and total 26 points with three game-winning goals (this, despite having his sea-

Evander Kane's athletic parents were extremely influential in getting him and his two sisters involved in sports. His mom, Sheri, was a professional volleyball player and his father, Perry, was an amateur boxer who played a bit of hockey as well. Kane — who was named after his father's favorite boxer, Evander Holyfield — will readily admit that it was his father's training influence and emphasis on fundamentals and conditioning that allowed him to truly excel. Kane's father would spend long hours with him in the boxing ring and he was constantly encouraged to practice his skating, puckhandling and shooting skills. Today, the 6-foot-2, 195-pound Kane has many great attributes to his game, but the one that stands out the most is the confidence he has to handle and shoot the puck. During

son reduced to 66 games mostly due to injuries). Kane's second NHL season saw his numbers improve modestly, with 19 goals and 43 points in 67 games.

At the close of the 2010–11 season, the team left Atlanta and moved north to Winnipeg, Manitoba, where Kane experienced a rough transition to his new surroundings. At one point, stories were even making the rounds that he did not like his new city or his coach (Claude Noel). Kane denied the rumors and promptly went out and played some great hockey for the re-established Winnipeg Jets. He had 12 goals and 19 points in the first 24 games of the season and went on to score 30 goals in total, which was more than any player on the team.

Kane sees himself as a power forward and few could argue with that assessment. He wants to improve each time he plays but he also knows he must be more consistent if he is to be a truly elite player. Kane has all the tools necessary to be a star in the NHL for many years to come, and

he should be secure in the knowledge that, on a nightly basis, he is the most important young player in the Jets' lineup. Indeed, the Jets will need Kane at the top of his game if they hope to make the playoffs any time soon.

- ▶ Drafted 4th overall by the Atlanta Thrashers in 2009
- ▶ Scored 14 goals as rookie in 2009–10
- ▶ Set single-season highs in goals (30) and points (57) in 2011–12
- ▶ Posted a plus-11 mark for the 2011–12 season
- ▶ Recorded 63 goals and 126 points in 213 career games

CAREER HIGHLIGHTS

WESTERN CONFERENCE TEAM STARS

The best of the Central, Northwest and Pacific.

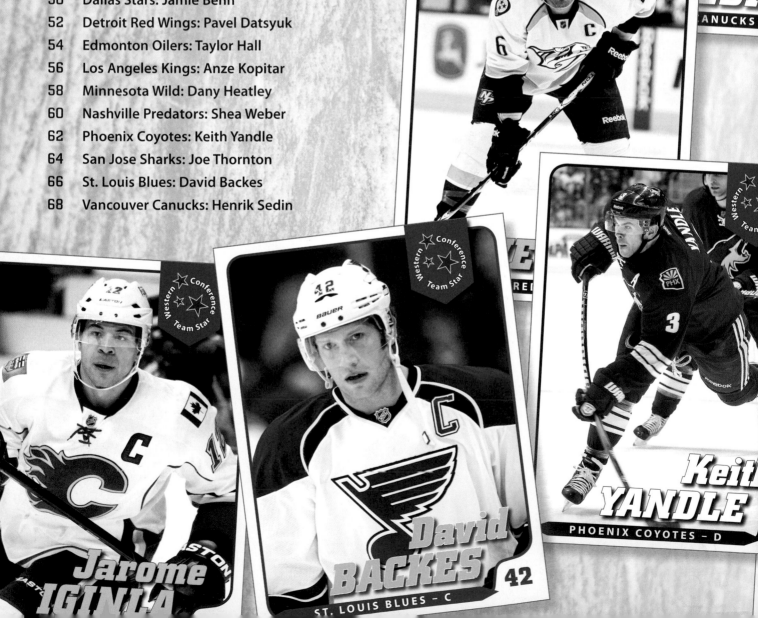

Western Conference Team Star

Western Conference Team Star

Western Conference Team Star

Conference Team Star

Western Conference Team Star

Western Conference Team Star

Matt
DUCHENE
COLORADO AVALANCHE – C
9

Conference Team Star

Western Conference Team Star

Western Conference Team Star

Jonathan
TOEWS

Dany
HEATLEY
MINNESOTA WILD – LW

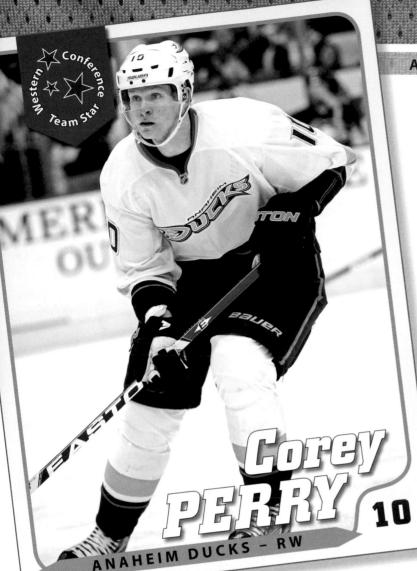

Corey
PERRY 10
ANAHEIM DUCKS – RW

Oceanic of the Quebec Major Junior League in the final.

At the age of 20 Perry was promoted to the Portland Pirates of the American Hockey League for the 2005–06 season. His 34 points in 19 games prompted Anaheim to promote him to the big league team before the season was out, and he and Ryan Getzlaf (a player also taken in the first round of the 2003 draft by Anaheim) came of age together in the NHL. The second year players both played pivotal roles during the 2006–07 season, and Perry scored 17 times in the regular season and then recorded another 15 points in 21 playoff games. Anaheim rolled over the Ottawa Senators in the Stanley Cup final by taking the series in just five games. At the final buzzer Perry threw his gloves in the air and waited anxiously to lift the silver trophy over his head. His dream of lifting the Stanley Cup came true in only his second pro season.

Perry can crash and bang with the best of them and he likes to place himself in and around the crease. At 6-foot-3 and 212 pounds, he is a hard body for defenders to move, and he isn't afraid of getting dirty in order to score goals. He can be reckless, however, and that has cost him. He recorded 127 penalty minutes in 2011–12 — the fifth straight year he has been over the 100 mark — and he can be careless with his stick and that draws the attention of the referees far too often.

Prior to the 2010–11 season, the right-winger had never scored more than 32 goals in one season. However, in the last 16 games of the 2010–11 season, Perry scored 19 times — five of which were game-winners — to bring his season total to 50. He was the only player in the NHL to hit the magic number that season, and the next highest goal scorer only totaled 45. Perry's great year, which included 98 points and a league leading 11 game-winning goals, was recognized with a spot on the First All-Star Team and the Hart Memorial Trophy as league MVP. The only downside to the season was

P erry was born in the small town of Peterborough, Ontario, where he enjoyed a pretty simple upbringing. In the winter he played hockey and in the summer he enjoyed all the water sports that the area offered. The London Knights of the Ontario Hockey League selected Perry in 2001 after coming off a minor hockey midget year that saw him collect 115 points in 64 games. He arrived in London weighing only 160 pounds. His first two years produced seasons of 59 and 78 points and his energizing style got him selected in the first round of the 2003 NHL entry draft by Anaheim, 28th overall. His final year of junior saw Perry collect 130 points while playing a major role for the Knights, who romped to the 2005 Memorial Cup championship, defeating Sidney Cosby's Rimouski

Anaheim's early exit from the playoffs at the hands of the Nashville Predators in the first round.

Perry came back to earth a little in 2011–12, scoring 37 times and adding 23 assists for 60 points — good enough for second in team scoring behind veteran Teemu Selanne. Yet the Ducks underperformed as a squad, and an extremely slow start to the season cost coach Randy Carlyle his job.

Positive steps were taken under the new coaching direction of Bruce Boudreau, but they could not recover fast enough to make the playoffs. It was the second time in three years the club failed to make the postseason after finishing with a pedestrian 34–36–12 record. The good news for Ducks fans is that Boudreau emphasizes a strong two-way game with offensive creativity, something that should suit Perry and the All-Star forwards on Anaheim's roster.

Hopes are that with Boudreau behind the bench the Anaheim attack will be reinvigorated and ready to reclaim the Cup.

CAREER HIGHLIGHTS

➤ Drafted 28th overall by the Anaheim Ducks in 2003

➤ Scored 50 goals and totaled 98 points in 2010–11

➤ Named winner of the Hart Memorial Trophy in 2011

➤ Named to the NHL First All-Star Team in 2011

➤ Recorded 205 goals and 429 points in 530 career games

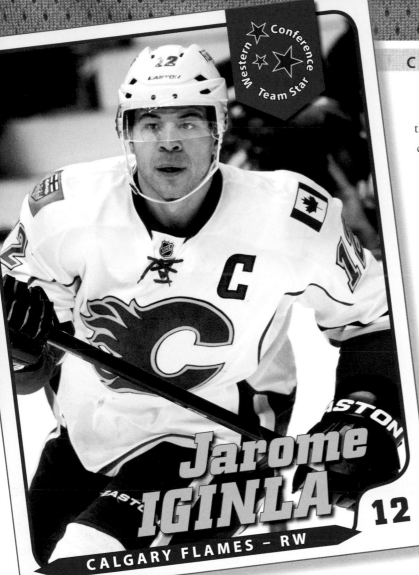

Western Conference
Team Star

Jarome
IGINLA
12
CALGARY FLAMES – RW

the puck is put on the net. The Flames bench cleared as soon as the team realized it was Iginla who had, indeed, scored; the crowd also rewarded the franchise's best player with their trademark chant of "Ig-gy! Ig-gy!"

Iginla has been a member of the Calgary organization since he first played in the NHL in 1996–97. With his 500th goal, he became just the 15th player in league history to score 500 goals for one team, joining such NHL luminaries as Wayne Gretzky (Edmonton Oilers), Joe Sakic (Quebec Nordiques/Colorado Avalanche) and Steve Yzerman (Detroit Red Wings), all of whom played against Iginla over the course of their great careers. The only other member of the Flames franchise who scored his 500th goal while wearing the team jersey was Lanny McDonald, but he also played for the Toronto Maple Leafs and the Colorado Rockies before he came to Calgary. McDonald was elected to the Hall of Fame when his career ended, and there is little doubt that Iginla will join him.

At the end of the 2011–12 season, Iginla held just about every Flames record, including: most seasons played (15), most games played (1,188), most career goals (516) and most career points (1,073). When Iginla scored his 500th goal, it was his 80th game-winner for the team, and this achievement in itself illustrates not only that the right-winger can fill the net, but also that he can do so in meaningful situations. Further, he has scored 253 goals on home ice and 263 on the road — a nearly even split — which shows that the highly respected Iginla plays the game the same way no matter where he is on the schedule.

The best part of the 2011–12 season for Calgary Flames captain Jarome Iginla came during a Saturday-night home game against the Minnesota Wild on January 7, 2012. This game saw Iginla, the face of the Calgary franchise for many years, become the 42nd player in NHL history to score 500 goals. The milestone was hit in the third period of Calgary's 3–1 win over the Wild, and the fact that Iginla scored No. 500 on home ice made the occasion that much sweeter.

Iginla was the first to concede that his shot from the boards that deflected off two opposing players before skipping past Minnesota goaltender Niklas Backstrom wasn't the prettiest of goals. It was actually a shot Backstrom might have normally saved, but as all good goal-scorers know, great things sometimes happen when

The Calgary Flames were not the original team to draft Iginla — that foresight went to the Dallas Stars who took him 11th overall in 1995. Dallas, however, eventually made a strong pitch for Joe Nieuwendyk, a star center for the Flames, and in order to complete the deal in December 1995, Dallas had to give Calgary the rights to Iginla. And yes, Nieuwendyk did help the Stars win the Stanley Cup in 1999, but the Flames have never regretted their trade. In fact, Iginla and Calgary came close to winning their own Stanley Cup final in 2004, but were edged out by the Tampa Bay Lightning after seven games.

The Flames have never been quite the same since their run for the Cup in 2004, and while coaches and managers have come and gone, Iginla's presence has been constant, and that has been a good thing for all involved. Flames management has never shown any interest in trading the 6-foot-1, 207-pound, Edmonton-born Iginla and he has never shown any desire to leave. Calgary, however, has not made the postseason in three years and has not won a playoff round since 2004, facts that might be starting to wear on the 34-year-old Iginla, who still had an impressive season in 2011–12 with 32 goals and

35 assists in 82 games. The year before (2010–11) saw him score 43 goals and total 86 points, both of which are indications that he is still an extremely productive player.

Nevertheless, some players simply belong in one sweater and one sweater only, and no matter where Iginla finishes his career, the flaming "C" will always be his heart and soul.

> Drafted 11th overall by the Dallas Stars in 1995
> Won the Art Ross Trophy in 2001–02 with 96 points
> Two-time winner of the Maurice Richard Trophy
> Three-time NHL First Team All-Star
> Recorded 516 goals and 1,073 points in 1,188 career games

CAREER HIGHLIGHTS

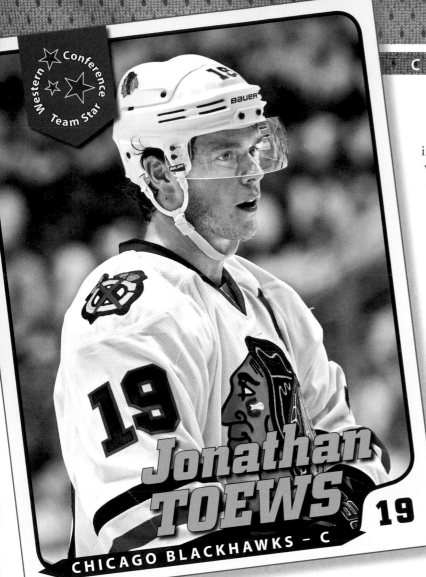

Western Conference
Team Star

Jonathan TOEWS 19

CHICAGO BLACKHAWKS – C

Chicago Blackhawks center Jonathan Toews may be the most complete player in the NHL. Sure, there are others who may fit the bill — like Pavel Datsyuk and Sidney Crosby — but Toews excels at so many aspects of the game that he outshines everyone else. First, he plays in all three zones of the rink and is as good a checker as he is a playmaker; he's also effective at even strength, with the man advantage or killing penalties. Second, he is exceptional at face-offs (one of the most important skills in the game, and something that is usually dominated by veterans). Third, he knows when to put his team on his shoulders — the leadership skills of "Captain Serious" are on par with players like Steve Yzerman and Mark Messier, two of the best captains to ever lace up skates.

Toews is just 23 years old, but his accomplishments in hockey are already legendary. The native of Winnipeg, Manitoba, has won two gold medals with Team Canada at the 2006 and 2007 World Junior Championships, was named to the NHL's All-Rookie Team in 2008, helped Canada to a gold medal at the 2010 Winter Olympics, and won a Stanley Cup the same year as his Olympic gold! During that playoff Toews recorded 22 points in 22 games and took home the Conn Smythe Trophy as playoff MVP. The Cup the Blackhawks won in 2010 was the Windy City's first in 49 years.

The Stanley Cup triumph was not the first time Toews had been a winning captain. When he was just nine years old and in Atom-level hockey in 1995, he captained his team to the city championship in Winnipeg. There are not many Atom-level teams that designate one captain for the entire year, but Toews and leadership just seem to go together.

In Chicago, the 6-foot-2, 209-pound Captain Serious is known for his very strict approach to the game. If things are not going well, Toews will sit and analyze what went wrong and figure out how to do it better. He gets teased strongly by his Chicago teammates, who see their leader as someone who acts much older than his years. But that is because Toews is extremely focused on what he wants to accomplish. He admitted he could not sleep the night before the last game of the 2010 Stanley Cup final because he kept imagining how it would feel if the Blackhawks won the championship. He then went out and set up Chicago's first tally of the game. The Philadelphia Flyers did a good job of containing Toews during the Cup final, but their added pressure on him underscores the respect the opposition has in him.

Despite the Blackhawks restructuring the lineup over the last couple of years, the offensive attack of Toews, Marian Hossa, Patrick Sharp and Patrick Kane has stayed intact, and defensemen Duncan Keith and Brent Seabrook are also still the mainstays on the blueline.

Since winning the Cup, Toews and his crew have suffered first round losses in both the 2011 and 2012 post-seasons. However, Toews enjoyed his career best regular season campaign in 2010–11, during which he earned 76 points (32 goals and 44 assists). He was on his way to another excellent season in 2011–12 — registering points at nearly a point-per-game pace — when injuries limited him to just 59 games. (Toews uses his body very willingly and is not afraid of contact in the least, but he might be a little undersized to take a constant beating.)

When Toews was a youngster he admired Joe Sakic of the Colorado Avalanche. Sakic also played center and he was an understated but very effective leader. Sakic won two Stanley Cups during his brilliant career. Toews likes to lead in a similar fashion — not flashy or abrasive, yet consistently determined to get the job done well. Toews, chosen third overall in 2006, looks to lead the Blackhawks to another Stanley Cup very soon and thereby matching the championship total of his childhood hero.

- Drafted 3rd overall by the Chicago Blackhawks in 2006
- Named captain of the Blackhawks in 2008
- Member of Stanley Cup–winning Blackhawks team in 2010
- Winner of the Conn Smythe Trophy in 2010
- Recorded 144 goals and 324 points in 361 games

CAREER HIGHLIGHTS

Matt DUCHENE 9
COLORADO AVALANCHE – C

When Matt Duchene scored his first NHL goal it came against goaltender Chris Osgood of the Detroit Red Wings, whom he had watched play for the Adirondack Red Wings in the American Hockey League when his uncle, Newell Brown, coached that club. That Duchene's first NHL goal happened against Osgood was a nice homage to the influences found in his early career. His entire family was also in attendance that day, which made the moment that much more memorable.

Duchene was just four years old when he started play-ing hockey for the Haliburton Huskies in his hometown of Haliburton, Ontario. He was also able to develop his skills in the driveway of his home when his father, Vince, decided to put up some boards so Duchene and

his friends could practice. Fishing line was eventually used as "mesh" behind the net, and in shop class at school, Duchene made a goalie out of sheet metal and wood in order to give him a target to beat with his shot. As further conditioning, his at-home rink was used year-round and he often improved his physical game while working out with childhood friend Cody Hodgson (who was a first-round pick of the Vancouver Canucks in 2008).

Overall, Duchene had a strong network helping him with his hockey development. His father, a former goaltender, helped mold Duchene's shot and awareness, and he had more than his share of advice given to him from Brown, who was a member of the Memorial Cup champion Cornwall Royals in 1980 and who was also an assistant coach with the Anaheim Ducks in 2009–10.

Duchene placed further positive influences on his career in the role models he chose, such as NHL superstar Joe Sakic of the Colorado Avalanche. A classy player, Sakic was a two-time Stanley Cup winner with 625 goals and 1,641 points to his credit. Brown even managed to get Sakic to sign a Colorado sweater, which he gave to Duchene, who promptly framed it and put it up on his wall. The Avalanche became Duchene's favorite team and as a sign of his devotion to the team, he would practice drawing its logo. Like many young hockey players, Duchene dreamed of wearing an NHL uniform, and he started on the road to fulfilling that hope when he played major junior hockey for the Brampton Battalion of the Ontario Hockey League (OHL).

It was on this team that he joined up once again with his good friend Hodgson. The pair produced two great years in Brampton, with Duchene scoring 61 goals in 121 regular-season games but saving his best play for the 2009 playoffs, where he had 14 goals and 26 points in 21 postseason games, all of which helped the Battalion to the OHL final. The timing of his most impressive performance as junior could not have been

better because it was at this point that he became eligible for the 2009 NHL entry draft. Duchene was happy to be selected by the Avalanche with the third pick, and the Denver-based club was thrilled to land the left-winger.

Duchene's career with the Avalanche began when he was 18 years old, and he played in 81 games as a rookie in 2009–10, scoring 24 times and adding 31 assists to lead his team in scoring with 54 points. He also helped his club secure a postseason spot by scoring a shootout winner against the Vancouver Canucks with just four games remaining in the season. Colorado was eventually ousted in six games by the San Jose Sharks, and even though Duchene didn't score, he contributed three assists.

CAREER HIGHLIGHTS

➤ Drafted 3rd overall by the Colorado Avalanche in 2009

➤ Named to NHL All-Rookie Team in 2010

➤ Scored 24 goals in NHL rookie season

➤ Scored 27 times in second season with the Avalanche

➤ Recorded 65 goals and 150 points in 219 career games

Duchene's high point to date came in his second season when he scored 27 times and totaled 67 points in 80 games. The 2011–12 campaign, however, was a tough one for the left-winger as injuries limited him to only 58 games and 28 points. But, at just 21 years old, the Avalanche will look for Duchene to bounce back for 2012–13.

Additionally, the good news for Duchene is that the Avalanche has a wealth of great young players, such as Ryan O'Reilly, Gabriel Landeskog, Paul Stastny, Erik Johnson and goalie Semyon Varlamov, to build its team around. Colorado should be a consistent playoff contender in upcoming seasons, and a healthy Duchene is expected to be a strong contributor.

Jack JOHNSON

COLUMBUS BLUE JACKETS – D   7

Selected third overall by the Carolina Hurricanes in the 2005 NHL entry draft, Johnson was traded before ever playing his first NHL game. When he and the Hurricanes could not reach a contract agreement the team quickly shipped him to the Los Angeles Kings. Rather than joining the Kings right away, Johnson stayed at the University of Michigan, playing the 2005–06 and 2006–07 campaigns as a Wolverine. In his two collegiate seasons Johnson scored a total of 26 goals and notched 71 points in 74 games.

Johnson got his first real test as a rookie with the Kings during the 2007–08 season, appearing in 74 games and recording 11 points. Although his defensive game was lacking, Johnson's very good offensive numbers impressed the Kings' management. He earned 36 points in 2009–10 and 42 the following season. In January 2011 the Kings decided to make a long-term investment in Johnson and signed him for $30.5 million over seven years. It looked like he was going to be in Los Angeles for quite some time.

Come the 2011–12 regular season, though, things were not going so well. Los Angeles was having a terrible time scoring goals and the Kings' general manager, Dean Lombardi, decided he needed a scoring center. He landed just that by trading Johnson and a future first-round draft selection for embattled center Jeff Carter from the Columbus Blue Jackets.

Moving Johnson was not an easy decision. The sturdy defenseman was having a decent year with 24 points after 61 games with the Kings, but team management believed they could get by without him in order to add some offense from Carter. As soon as the deal was done Johnson did his best to forget about Los Angeles and focus on his new team instead. He was given Carter's No. 7 sweater and the Blue Jackets even offered a nameplate swap to those fans who had a jersey with Carter's name on it. Johnson immediately felt at home in Ohio and many hockey observers felt the Columbus squad had made a very good deal indeed.

NHL players react to trades in very different ways. Some get upset by them, some welcome them as a new challenge and others just accept that they're a part of playing in the world's greatest hockey league. As for Jack Johnson, the 25-year-old defenseman has already been traded twice in his still budding career and has accepted each trade as the best move for his future.

Born in Indianapolis, Indiana, Johnson is a Midwestern boy at heart. When he was traded from the Los Angeles Kings (who went on to win the Stanley Cup) to the Columbus Blue Jackets (who finished with the worst record in the league) in the latter part of the 2011–12 season he didn't get upset. Rather, he felt like he was going home to his Midwestern roots.

Johnson played the final 21 games of the 2011–12 season for the Blue Jackets, scoring four goals and adding 10 assists for a total of 14 points. More importantly, he was a plus 5 for his new team while he had always been a high minus player for the Kings (which was part of the reason Los Angeles was willing to move him out).

Johnson enjoys being the premier defenseman and will get that opportunity in Columbus, though he'll have to work on becoming more defensively responsible as the goaltending situation in Columbus is not nearly as strong as it was in L.A. Without a premier puckstopper to clean up some of his mistakes, Johnson's career minus trend is sure to continue, something the struggling Columbus team can't afford to have happen. With the departure of Columbus' franchise star Rick Nash in the 2012 off-season, Johnson will be expected to step up and

become a leader for the Blue Jackets both in the dressing room and on the ice. He gained some good experience in this regard when he was named captain of the United States National Team at the 2012 World Championships.

Although Johnson missed the Kings' exciting playoff run in the 2012 postseason, he is ready to help launch a new era in Columbus and make the Midwest proud.

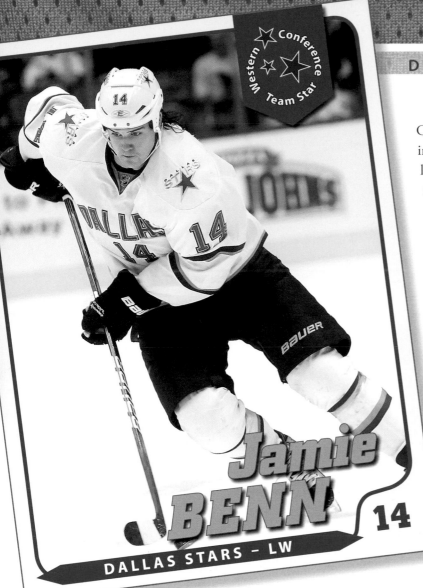

Western Conference Team Star

Jamie BENN 14

DALLAS STARS – LW

Canada at the World Junior Hockey Championships in Ottawa, Ontario, and while he was playing on a line with Tyler Ennis and Brett Sonne, Benn registered four goals and two assists in six games.

He returned to Kelowna to produce 82 points in 56 games in his final year of junior hockey, which was also the season in which the Rockets captured the WHL title and a berth in the Memorial Cup. Benn's scoring prowess was displayed in the Rockets' round-robin game against the Drummondville Voltigeurs — he scored four times (once on the power play, once shorthanded and twice at even-strength) to give his team a 6–4 win and the chance to move on to the final game. The dream season ended, however, when the Rockets fell to the powerhouse Windsor Spitfires. Nevertheless, Benn's output of nine points in four games was enough to claim the Ed Chynoweth Trophy that is awarded to the tournament's leading scorer. At the season's end, Benn was also named to the WHL West First All-Star Team.

Benn joined the Stars in 2009–10, and was one of only three players to suit up for all 82 games. Dallas failed to qualify for the playoffs that year, though, so Benn was loaned to the Stars' American Hockey League affiliate in Cedar Park, Texas. Registering 26 points in 24 games, Benn finished third among playoff scorers. Once again, however, his team was runner-up, as the Texas Stars lost the Calder Cup final in six games to the Hershey Bears.

Benn avoided the sophomore jinx by repeating his 22-goal output in 2010–11, and a pugilistic side to his game became evident as he engaged in four fights over the course of the campaign; Benn's most memorable scrap occurred in a mid-season game versus the Calgary Flames when he took on their captain, Jarome Iginla.

The following 2011–12 season was a breakthrough year for Benn, and it began with a game-winning goal in the Stars' first outing of the year against the Chicago Blackhawks. As an encore, Benn followed up with a

E very NHL team hopes to find a gem in the late rounds of the draft, and in 2007, this expectation was no different. From that year's late selections came three players who now look poised to become solid NHL contributors: Wayne Simmonds (61st overall), Carl Gunnarsson (194th overall) and Jamie Benn (129th overall). By the end of the 2011–12 season, each player had played over 180 games, and while all three are undoubtedly talented, Benn has emerged as a consistent scorer who has three seasons of 22 goals or more with the Dallas Stars.

The native of Victoria, British Columbia, first starred as a junior in his home province, where he played for the Kelowna Rockets of the Western Hockey League (WHL). Then, in 2009, he was selected to play for Team

highlight-reel goal the next week against the Columbus Blue Jackets. On the play, Benn received the puck at the Blue Jackets' blue line, cut from the right side boards into the middle of the ice and then weaved through four Columbus skaters, including star forward Rick Nash. A helpless Steve Mason could only watch as Benn became an overnight sensation by finding the net to cap off the play.

In early January, Benn reeled off three consecutive multi-point games to be named an NHL First Star of the Week for the first time in his career. Then, at the end of the month, he represented Dallas at the league's All-Star Game in Ottawa. Benn's weekend was highlighted by claiming the shooting accuracy event in the Skills Competition, hitting four of five targets in 10.2 seconds to surpass his closest challenger, the Philadelphia Flyers' Matt Read.

The Stars played well for most of 2011–12 under new coach Glen Gulutzan, but just missed the play-offs with a 42–35–4 record. General manager Joe Nieuwendyk had done a remarkable job of putting a team together, and now that ownership issues have been settled, the Stars will be able to spend more to make the team better.

A good thing about Dallas missing the postseason was that Benn had a chance to play for Team Canada at the World Championships. The international experience allowed him to show off his skills and strength on a wider ice surface, and he will come back to Dallas a better player who's ready for the 2012–13 season.

> Drafted 129th overall by Dallas in 2007

> Has scored 22 or more goals in each of his first three NHL seasons

> Scored four short–handed goals in 2010–11

> Recorded a career best 63 points (26G, 37A) in 2011–12

> Recorded 70 goals and 160 points in 222 career games

CAREER HIGHLIGHTS

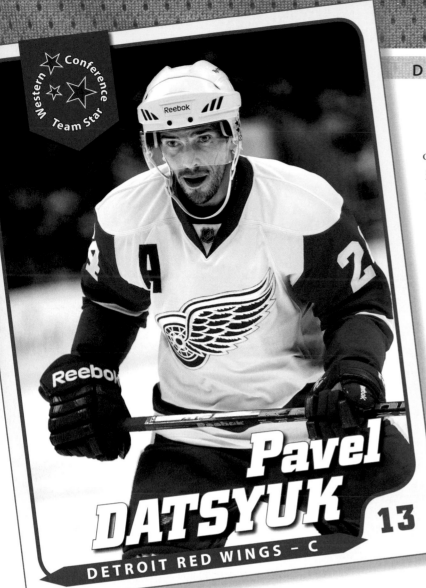

Western Conference Team Star

Pavel **DATSYUK** 13

DETROIT RED WINGS – C

The Detroit Red Wings selected Datsyuk 171st overall in 1998, and he was available at such a low spot in the draft because of his relatively small size. The fact that he had never played junior hockey in North America also scared teams away. The Red Wings, too, were not sure what they had in Datsyuk, but upon coming to the U.S., the highly skilled forward never spent a day in the minor leagues.

Datsyuk had a taste of early NHL success when he joined the Red Wings for the 2001–02 campaign after playing in the Russian professional league. He played in 70 games as a rookie, recorded 11 goals and 35 points and chipped in 3 goals and 3 assists in the playoffs, in which Detroit won the Stanley Cup.

After their championship win in 2002, however, the Red Wings underwent changes on their roster and Datsyuk was suddenly in the right spot to assert himself as a top-six forward. During the 2003–04 season, Datsyuk started to show his offensive abilities, as he and legendary sniper Brett Hull shared the club's lead in points with 68. Since then, Datsyuk has had 87 points or greater five times, and he has twice reached his career high of 97.

Datsyuk goes about his duties in a clean and determined manner, which is a routine that has earned him a well-deserved reputation for his sportsmanlike play. He sets a good example of how the game should be played, and his success is a reminder that a player does not have to be large and outwardly physical in order to excel in hockey.

Datsyuk has earned only one All-Star nomination (to the Second All-Star Team in 2008–09) and while he deserves more berths, his pass-first attitude and low goal totals have probably contributed to his lack of All-Star love. Like a true NHLer, though, Datsyuk is able to elevate his game come playoff time, where he has 61 points in 126 career games and where he is at his shutdown best. His 23 points in 22 postseason games were integral to the Red Wings winning the Cup in 2008, as

I f there was ever any doubt about how good a hockey player Pavel Datsyuk is, naysayers need look no further than the back-to-back seasons in which he won both the Lady Byng Memorial and Frank J. Selke trophies (2007–08 and 2008–09). True, the Lady Byng award (for most sportsmanlike behavior) and the Selke trophy (given to the top defensive forward) don't have profiles as large as those given to the Hart Memorial Trophy or Art Ross Trophy, but Datsyuk's honors clearly show that he is not only a clean player, but that he is capable of playing well defensively without taking needless penalties. Indeed, the 5-foot-11, 194-pound Russia-born center, who has registered only 186 penalty minutes in 732 career games, is perhaps the top two-way forward in the game.

was his role in shutting down the Pittsburgh Penguins' top scorers in the final.

Along with his gentlemanly play and defensive awareness, Datsyuk has done well at the NHL level because he is a highly skilled player who has superior puckhandling ability and vision. He is exceptional at spotting an open teammate, and his deft maneuvering wins him many loose pucks — it also allows him to keep the puck in many situations where other players would certainly lose it. But, despite these abilities, everyone has a weak spot, and if there was one skill Datsyuk could exploit more regularly, it would likely be his pinpoint accurate shot because if he was able to let it go more often, he would certainly find the back of the net more than he does now, which is never a bad thing.

However, it's not as if Datsyuk is lacking in playing time — the 34 year old recently added a World Hockey Championship to his illustrious résumé by helping Russia win the title in 2012. At the time, he said it was like winning the Stanley Cup, and while the Red Wings have made the postseason for 21 straight seasons, Datsyuk likely hopes to experience that feeling once again when the team brings home its next championship.

➤ Drafted 171st overall by the Detroit Red Wings in 1998

➤ Member of two Stanley Cup–winning Red Wings teams

➤ Four-time winner of the Lady Byng Memorial Trophy

➤ Three-time winner of the Frank J. Selke Trophy

➤ Recorded 240 goals and 718 points in 732 career games

CAREER HIGHLIGHTS

Western Conference Team Star

Taylor **HALL**

EDMONTON OILERS – LW

4

Hall showed he could more than hold his own in the demanding and competitive league.

Before his junior career was over, Hall and the Spitfires won two Memorial Cups (in back-to-back seasons in 2008 and 2009), and Hall produced 280 points (123 goals and 157 assists) in just three OHL seasons. He credited his coach, former NHL player Bob Boughner, for helping him to develop the skills he needed to make the NHL.

As the 2009 NHL entry draft approached, most pundits predicted that Hall or Tyler Seguin would be selected first overall. The speculations were spot-on, and on June 25, 2010, the Edmonton Oilers, who held the first pick, chose Hall first overall.

The Oilers were looking to Hall in much the same way they looked to Wayne Gretzky when the team joined the NHL in 1979. At the time, they knew the future of the franchise rested on Gretzky's shoulders, and now, a similar expectation rests on Hall's conscience. To presume anyone could ever replicate what "The Great One" did in Edmonton would be foolish, but if anyone is going to come close, the hope is that it will be the 6-foot-1, 194-pound Hall. The sublimely talented left-winger is the building block that the Oilers will use as the foundation of what they hope will be a new dynasty.

As a rookie in 2010–11, Hall was in a position to compete for the Calder Memorial Trophy, but a late-season injury ended his hopes of being named rookie of the year. Up until that point, however, he had 22 goals and 42 points in 66 games while playing for one of the worst teams in the entire league. In fact, in a game that season against the Atlanta Thrashers, he took a total of nine shots on net and scored three power-play goals, all in one period. Hall got off to a good start in the 2011–12 season as well and had 30 points in his first 34 games, but the second half of his year was ruined once again by a shoulder injury that required surgery.

Hall's game is really all about his great skating skills.

Taylor Hall was born in Calgary, Alberta, and while this is where he started playing minor hockey, when he turned 13, his family made the decision to move to Kingston, Ontario, where Hall's mother Kim had relatives. Hall's father Steve, on the other hand, was a professional football player in the Canadian Football League as well as a later member of the Canadian national bobsleigh team. Hall, however, was far too interested in hockey to give any significant thought to following in his father's footsteps. After playing the 2006–07 season with the Greater Kingston Junior Frontenacs and scoring 44 goals in just 29 games, Hall was drafted by the Windsor Spitfires of the Ontario Hockey League (OHL). He began playing for Windsor when he was just 15 years old, and despite his youth,

He has a wide and long stride that can get him around defenders with considerable speed. He shows no fear in attacking with the puck and is more than capable of finishing the play when he finds himself in a scoring position. His energetic, up-tempo style lifts fans out of their seats and makes him worth the price of admission. Nevertheless, the fearless nature of Hall's approach to playing the game might have to be altered slightly if he is to survive and avoid yearly injuries. This will not be easy because Hall is an inspired and passionate player who wants his team to do well. The Oilers, however, have to pull their weight, too, and they must do more as a team to surround their star with talent, which means that the large number of Edmonton players who were selected high in the first round must begin to pay dividends. If everything can come together as the team's young players mature, the Oilers and their fans can hold out hope that another Gretzky-like dynasty is on the horizon.

- ➤ Drafted 1st overall by the Edmonton Oilers in 2010
- ➤ Led the OHL in points with 106 in 2009–10
- ➤ Winner of two Memorial Cups with the Windsor Spitfires
- ➤ Scored 20 or more goals in his first two NHL seasons
- ➤ Recorded 49 goals and 95 points in 126 career games

CAREER HIGHLIGHTS

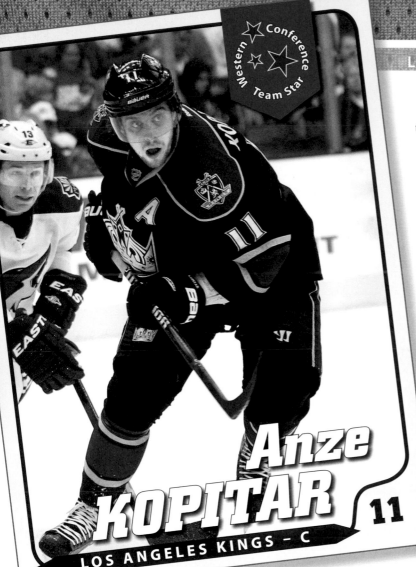

Western Conference Team Star

Anze KOPITAR 11
LOS ANGELES KINGS – C

The opening game of the 2012 Stanley Cup final was tied 1–1 at the end of regulation time. Neither the Los Angeles Kings nor the New Jersey Devils were giving up much in the way of scoring opportunities. The teams were feeling each other out and it was a tight checking game with plenty of blocked shots and not much flow.

Then suddenly, after eight minutes of overtime, Los Angeles right-winger Justin Williams found forward Anze Kopitar with a breakaway pass, and Kopitar was in all alone on Devils goalie Martin Brodeur. The Kings couldn't have hoped for a better player to be in that position. Kopitar cradled the puck and moved in on the net, showing Brodeur the puck and then quickly faking to the goaltender's glove side. Brodeur went down to

the ice and Kopitar deked across the front of the net to Brodeur's blocker side. Kopitar waited and waited until he was at the side of the net before sending the puck across the line under a sprawling Brodeur. It was without question the most important and dramatic goal Kopitar had ever scored and it gave Los Angeles the upper hand in the Cup final.

The championship win for the Kings capped off a great season for Kopitar, who led his team in points for the fifth straight season, with 25 goals and 51 assists for 76 points. During the playoffs, Kopitar was tied with teammate Dustin Brown for the lead in scoring with 20 points in 20 games, making him a serious candidate for the Conn Smythe Trophy (though that coveted award went to teammate Jonathan Quick for his stellar goaltending).

If hockey fans were not aware of Kopitar before the 2012 postseason, they certainly became aware of the 6-foot-3, 227-pound center by the time the playoffs were over. The Kings have so rarely advanced in the playoffs that the team's players often operate in almost complete anonymity on the West Coast. However, 24-year-old Kopitar and a number of his young teammates just might keep the Kings in the front pages of the hockey news for some time to come.

In addition to his great hockey skills, Kopitar holds one other noteworthy distinction: he is the first and, thus far, only NHL player born in Slovenia. When Kopitar was born, the nation of his birth was still known as Yugoslavia, but with the collapse of the former federation in 1991 Slovenia became an independent state. In a nation of just over two million people, young Kopitar was one of few who wanted to become a professional hockey player. Most of the kids he grew up with wanted to play soccer or basketball, but Kopitar's father, Matjaz, was a former hockey player who had his son skating before he turned four years old.

Kopitar began playing in his hometown of Jesenice, a small industrial area, and dominated there with 196 points in 91 games at various levels of play. He moved to Sweden on his own at age 17 in order to play against better competition. He missed his family and often felt lonely, but the move paid off when the Los Angeles Kings took him 11th overall during the 2005 NHL entry draft.

A 19-year-old Kopitar made his debut in Los Angeles in 2006–07, producing 20 goals and 61 points in 72 games for what was then a rather weak team. He had 32 goals and 77 points in 82 regular-season games the next season, but slipped back a little in 2008–09, recording only 66 points.

The Kings were undergoing a major reconstruction and missed the playoffs each of Kopitar's first three seasons. During the summer of 2009, however, Kopitar dedicated himself to improving — and it showed. His strong effort in 2009–10 saw him earn a career high of

34 goals and 81 points. He also began to pay more attention to his defensive game and was a plus player for the first time ever (he has been a combined plus 43 over the last three NHL seasons).

Kopitar has impressed the Kings so much that they've signed him to a new seven-year contract worth $47.5 million. And California has now become home to Kopitar's entire family.

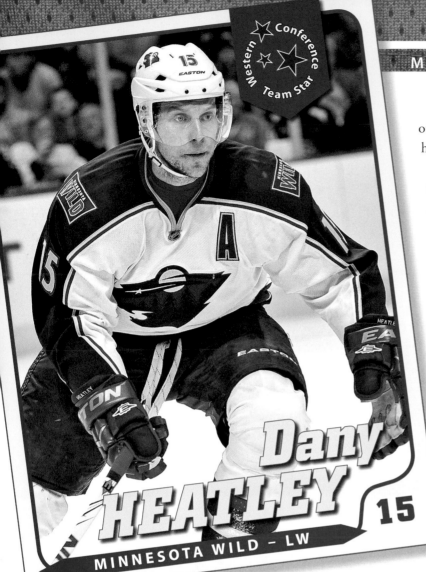

Western Conference Team Star

Dany **HEATLEY** 15

MINNESOTA WILD – LW

out of Atlanta. The team obliged his wishes by sending him to the Ottawa Senators for the 2005–06 season.

Heatley excelled in the Canadian capital, and over the next four seasons scored 50 goals twice. In 2007, he also contributed 22 points in 20 playoff games as the Senators made the Stanley Cup final. In the end, Ottawa succumbed to a superior team in the Anaheim Ducks, but for Heatley, it showed he could compete when it mattered most.

Two years later, in 2009, Heatley wanted out of Ottawa. Citing personal and professional reasons for the request, it was believed he did not see eye-to-eye with new-at-the-time bench boss Cory Clouston. Senators fans — and hockey fans, in general — reacted badly to Heatley's appeal, and the public-relations nightmare got worse when it was revealed that Heatley would not accept a deal with just any team; he wanted to go to a contending team, and because of this, famously vetoed a trade to the Edmonton Oilers.

Heatley eventually landed a deal with the San Jose Sharks, where he scored a respectable 65 goals in 162 games between the 2009–10 season and the 2010–11 season, but he could not recapture his 2007 playoff form and was less than stellar for the Sharks in the playoffs, scoring only five times in 32 games. Sharks general manager Doug Wilson (who was instrumental in bringing Heatley to the Western Conference) had hoped that the chemistry Heatley had experienced with San Jose's franchise players Joe Thornton and Patrick Marleau on Team Canada at the 2010 Winter Olympics would translate into success for the Sharks, but those plans didn't pan out, so Heatley was dealt to the Minnesota Wild.

Heatley said he was happy to go to the Wild, and in the early months of the 2011–12 season, Minnesota was the best team in the league. From November 13 to December 10, 2011, the Wild won 12 games and lost only twice, but injuries to key players Mikko Koivu and Devin Setoguchi derailed the team's playoff chances and as a result, the Wild went on a long losing skid. Under

For all his talents, Dany Heatley has not made things easy on himself. A proven goal-scorer, the talented but enigmatic left-winger has dealt with some supreme highs and lows since he was drafted second overall by the Atlanta Thrashers in 2000.

After joining the Thrashers, Heatley proved to be a popular teammate, and he topped off his debut NHL season by winning the Calder Memorial Trophy in 2001–02. Tragedy, however, soon struck on September 29, 2003, when Heatley was the driver in a car accident that eventually took the life of fellow Thrasher Dan Snyder. After the crash (for which Heatley was sentenced to three years of probation and community service), the Snyder family publicly forgave Heatley, but he still found it difficult to deal with the scrutiny and asked to be let

- ► Drafted 2nd overall by the Atlanta Thrashers in 2000
- ► Named winner of the Calder Memorial Trophy in 2002
- ► Scored 50 goals in two consecutive years with the Thrashers
- ► Scored 26 or more goals in nine NHL seasons
- ► Recorded 349 goals and 742 points in 751 career games

CAREER HIGHLIGHTS

the tutelage of new coach Mike Yeo, the Wild managed to finish the year with a 35–36–11 record, which was good enough for 81 points but not for the playoffs. This was the third straight year that the Wild took an early vacation.

As for Heatley himself, the 6-foot-4, 220-pound left-winger led the Wild in goals scored (24) and points (53) and was generally a good fit on the team. He can also still produce on the power play and can unload a decent amount of shots on goal (he had 238 in 2011–12, which doesn't exactly place him among the league's elite shooters but isn't far too off the mark, either). Further, Heatley averaged nearly 21 minutes of ice time per game, so perhaps with a few more shots and some increased offensive support from new teammate Zach Parise, fans can entertain the possibility of Heatley turning both his and his team's fortunes around.

Working hard to display more of this talent might also be in Heatley's best interests because Wild general manager Chuck Fletcher has shown he is not afraid to make changes on the ice and behind the bench. But, even with this being said, the truth of the matter is that Minnesota's current crop of young players will likely need veterans such as Heatley if the franchise wants a chance at hoisting the Stanley Cup.

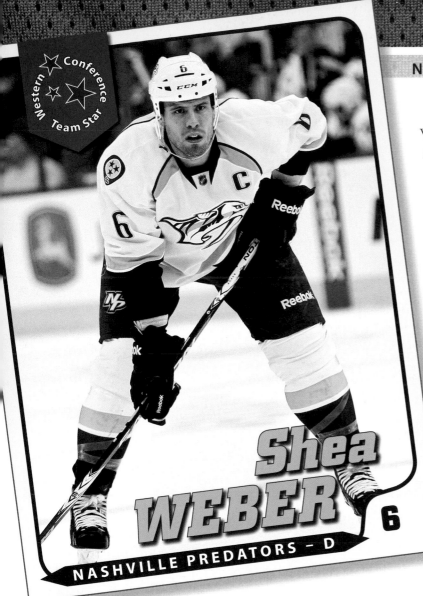

Western Conference Team Star

Shea WEBER

NASHVILLE PREDATORS – D

6

NASHVILLE PREDATORS

Wings, then lose the semifinal to the Phoenix Coyotes in just five games.

The reasons for Nashville's poor showing are varied, but it's clear that Weber, who had been a candidate for the James Norris Memorial Trophy, did not play up to his usual standard against the Coyotes (a team that played a similar style of hockey to the Predators).

Weber's offensive game is built around his great shot. Clocked at 103.4 miles per hour, it's a shot that no player — teammate or opponent — wants to be in the way of, and one that is especially effective on the power play, where Weber gets a little more space and time to pound the puck. In fact, 46 of Weber's 99 career goals to date have come from power plays.

Now entering the prime of his career, Weber is widely considered one of the best defensemen in the NHL. His all-around game is an impressive package of power, physical play, mobility and poise under pressure. He has used his 6-foot-4, 234-pound frame to deliver many bone-jarring but clean hits, and in his seven seasons has not once had more than 80 penalty minutes, collecting a total of just 369 minutes in 480 games. Weber's fast foot speed allows him to stay with his attackers one-on-one, guiding them toward the boards where he routinely stops them in their tracks. He did, however, show a nasty, undisciplined side in the 2012 playoffs when he rammed Detroit's Henrik Zetterberg into the glass headfirst, an unbecoming move for the typically poised captain.

Weber may not have been the largest boy growing up, but he eventually made it onto the Kelowna Rockets of the Western Hockey League, where he played for and won the Memorial Cup in 2004. He was also a key member of the gold medal–winning Canadian team at the 2005 World Junior Championship. The Toronto Maple Leafs' Dion Phaneuf was a fellow blue-liner on that junior squad and the two defensemen have often been compared, despite the fact that Phaneuf went ninth

The 2011–12 regular season and playoffs seemed like two entirely different seasons for Nashville Predators captain and defenseman Shea Weber. He scored 19 goals during the regular campaign — tying Erik Karlsson of the Ottawa Senators for the most goals by any defenseman in the NHL — and finished sixth among blue-liners in points, with 49. Weber posted a plus-21 rating and unleashed his bomb of a shot to score 10 power-play goals. Led by the versatile captain, Nashville won a club record 48 games and finished with 104 points.

In the playoffs, however, Weber managed only two goals and ended up a minus one for the postseason, which saw the Predators win the conference quarterfinal series against their longtime nemesis, the Detroit Red

overall at the 2003 entry draft while Weber was selected 49th.

Weber joined the NHL with the Nashville Predators in the 2005–06 season. His consistent play over the years made him a natural Team Canada selection for the 2010 Winter Olympics, where he had an exceptional tournament earning six points (including two goals) in seven games, winning gold and showing the entire hockey world how much his game had developed.

But can Weber lead the Predators to a Stanley Cup? During the 2012 off-season, the Philadelphia Flyers signed Weber (who was a restricted free agent at the time) to an offer sheet worth $110 million over 14 years. The Predators had just lost their No. 2 defender, Ryan Suter, to the Minnesota Wild via free agency, and popular opinion was that Nashville couldn't afford to let Weber walk too. There was much speculation about how the Predators would respond.

In the end, Nashville's general manager, David Poile,

> Drafted 49th overall by the Nashville Predators in 2003

> Two-time NHL First Team All-Star

> Named captain of the Predators in 2010

> Member of Canadian gold-medal-winning team at 2010 Winter Olympics

> Recorded 99 goals and 263 points in 480 career games

CAREER HIGHLIGHTS

decided Weber was worth the money and matched the offer sheet. Many called it the biggest decision in franchise history. With Weber secured in Nashville for the next 14 years, Poile will no doubt be working to keep his franchise player happy. Ultimately, that happiness must translate into success, meaning Shea Weber — and the Nashville Predators — must win a Stanley Cup in the next 14 years.

Keith YANDLE 3

PHOENIX COYOTES – D

By the time he was 18 years old Yandle was playing for his high school team, the Cushing Academy Penguins. He recorded 14 goals and a total of 54 points in just 34 games, and that attracted the attention of the Phoenix Coyotes who took him with the 105th pick of the 2005 entry draft. He then went to the Moncton Wildcats of the Quebec Major Junior Hockey League (QMJHL) and recorded 84 points in just 66 games during the 2005–06 season. Yandle was not only scoring, he was also a solid defender, posting a staggering plus-50 rating in a Quebec league known mostly for its potent offenses. That season Yandle performed well in the playoffs for Moncton, collecting 20 points in 21 games as the club, guided by former NHL coach Ted Nolan, beat the Quebec Remparts for its first QMJHL championship. The Wildcats also played host to the Memorial Cup tournament in 2006, and in a QMJHL final rematch against Quebec, Yandle's team could not repeat.

Following his fantastic 2005–06 campaign, the Coyotes sent the 6-foot-1, 205-pound defenseman from Moncton to their American Hockey League affiliate San Antonio. Yandle played a year and a half for the Rampage and recorded 48 points in 99 games, but the rigors of the professional game showed as he slipped to a minus-15 rating in his first season. He rebounded and was a plus-3 player when the Coyotes decided to give him a crack at the NHL. He played 42 games in the 2007–08 season and he has never looked back since.

Yandle has continued to develop as an NHL defenseman over the last six seasons. He is an offensive force from the blueline and has scored in double digits (12, 11 and 11) for the last three seasons. He pounds the puck at the net with great force and accuracy, but has an easy manner when handling the puck and is unafraid to take chances on the attack. In 2010–11 he had a breakout season, finishing with 59 points — it was a pleasant surprise for the Coyotes, and a shock to the rest of the league, as Phoenix overnight gained an A-level offensive

Boston-born defenseman Keith Yandle played competitive hockey from a young age and his father factored heavily into his sporting life. Yandle was encouraged to play a variety of sports and although hockey was his favorite, his father would not allow him to play during the summer. He wanted his son to take time off from hockey — to make sure hockey did not take over his son's life. So, Yandle played summer sports, and when September came around hockey was all he would think about.

As the youngest of three children, Yandle would often get hand-me-down equipment, but after he made friends with Chris Bourque, the son of legendary NHL defenseman Ray Bourque — one of Yandle's idols — he began getting hand-me-down sticks straight from the NHL.

defenseman. His point total dipped to 43 in 2011–12, but the Coyotes, as run by Dave Tippett, are hardly an offensive machine.

The Coyotes may play in anonymity in the Arizona desert, but they are making a name for themselves around the league, having made it into the playoffs for three consecutive years (2010 through 2012). In 2012, riding the hot goaltending of Mike Smith, the Coyotes made it all the way to the Western Conference final for the first time in franchise history. A date to play for the Stanley Cup was not to be, as the Los Angeles Kings dispatched them in five games.

Certainty is a hard thing to come by for a hockey player in the desert. Yandle's name has been bandied about more than once in the trade rumor mill, and as long as Phoenix survives without an owner, the talk will probably remain the same. Uncertainty also lies in the fate of the franchise, but, whether the team relocates or stays in the desert, two things are certain: both Yandle and the Coyotes are the real deal.

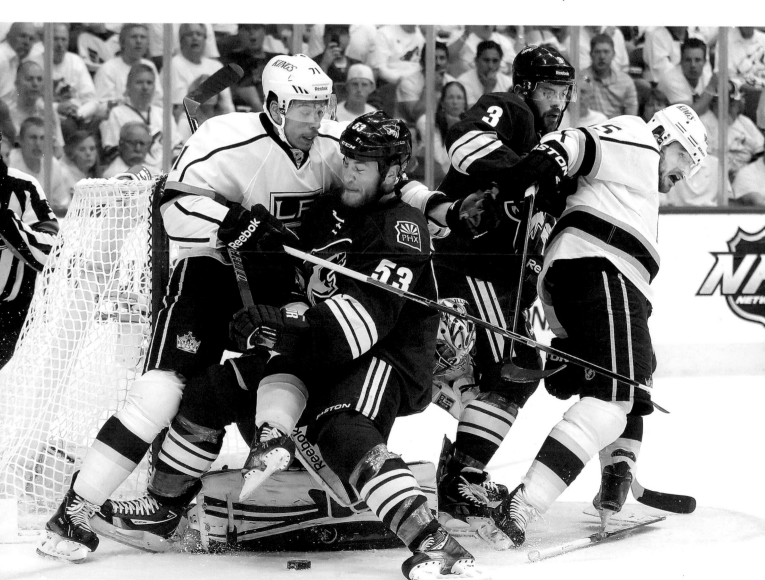

Western Conference Team Star

Joe THORNTON 19

SAN JOSE SHARKS – C

Sharks on November 30, 2005, he has played in 545 regular season games for the team and produced 624 points (155 goals, 469 assists) and his Sharks have never won less than 43 games in any season. Twice they have been the best team in the league. But all the regular season success in the world becomes less meaningful if you can't succeed in the playoffs, and that has been the downfall for the Sharks time and time again. While he still posts impressive totals in the playoffs, Thornton's 60 points in 79 playoff games is well shy of what is expected of the big centerman. In the meantime the Bruins went on to win the Stanley Cup in 2011, dismissing the long-held notion that they lost too much when they traded Thornton away.

Thornton has had some measure of success when competing in championship situations. He was the youngest member on Team Canada at the 1997 World Junior Championships, where he contributed two goals and two assists in seven games to help the Canadians win their fifth straight gold medal. But aside from that positive showing, even Thornton's most recent success as a member of the gold medal winning Canadian side at the 2010 Vancouver Olympics is somewhat misleading. He finished the tournament with one goal and one assist and a minus-one rating over seven games. It was a similar performance that he turned in while playing on the 2006 Olympic squad that finished a disappointing seventh. His numbers in that tournament were one goal and two assists over six games with a minus-one rating. Both performances were troublesome for a player who has aptly demonstrated he can dominate the game.

The knock on Thornton is that for a player of his size he should be more physical and play a more robust style of game. If he did, he would be able to back up his sublime skill with some grit, and that may help him get through rough patches, such as when he only scored 18 times in 2011–12. It may also help him lead the Sharks to the promised land.

Many players would give anything to have the career that Joe Thornton has enjoyed since he entered the NHL in the 1997–98 season. He was selected first overall by the Boston Bruins in the 1997 entry draft, and has thus far appeared in 1,077 NHL games in which he has collected 1,078 career points. The hulking 6-foot-4, 230-pound center nicknamed "Jumbo" has been nominated a team captain, an All-Star and the league MVP. He has not missed the playoffs since he was traded to the San Jose Sharks seven years ago, but there is one big "however" to Thornton's great career: he has yet to win a Stanley Cup. In fact, Thornton is yet to even make an appearance in the Stanley Cup final.

Since the Bruins traded Thornton to the San Jose

However, San Jose's playoff disappointments cannot be placed solely on the broad shoulders of Thornton. Teammate and alternate captain Patrick Marleau, who has been with the club for 14 seasons, has also had consistently fantastic regular seasons followed by below average and disappointing playoff performances. Other Sharks have come and gone, and also been ineffective when it matters most. Players like Dany Heatley, Evgeni Nabakov, Brent Burns and Martin Havlat have been unable to help San Jose succeed in the playoffs.

General Manager Doug Wilson has been much maligned in the media for refusing to trade his top two forwards, Thornton and Marleau. His reluctance originates in the raw talent of both of these stars, yet soon it would seem that if the Sharks don't make it to the Stanley Cup final, and Thornton and Marleau are still on the roster, that Wilson's job itself may be at stake.

The Sharks do have some good young players who can take the pressure off Thornton and Marleau — namely Joe Pavelski and Logan Couture. The hope is that with a little less pressure Thornton can harness his incredible skill when it matters most. If Thornton, Marleau, Pavelski and Couture — along with the other very talented Sharks — can put it all together come playoff time, this team could very easily help Thornton put to rest his playoff demons and quiet his naysayers.

CAREER HIGHLIGHTS

▶ Drafted 1st overall by the Boston Bruins in 1997

▶ Winner of the Art Ross Trophy for the 2005–06 season

▶ Named winner of the Hart Memorial Trophy in 2006

▶ Recorded 324 goals and 1,078 points in 1,077 games played

David
BACKES
42
ST. LOUIS BLUES – C

and 2001. The 17 year old then joined the United States Hockey League (USHL) and played briefly in Chicago before moving on to play in Lincoln, Nebraska. Backes' prolific goal-scoring in the USHL (70 goals in 112 games) got him into Minnesota State University where he further developed for three seasons while majoring in mechanical engineering.

Backes turned professional in 2005–06 and played for the Blues' American Hockey League farm team, the Peoria Rivermen, scoring 15 goals in 43 games over two years. As a rookie in the NHL in 2006–07, Backes scored 10 goals in 49 games and showed he could play a tough role in the league. He became a more effective player when the Blues switched him to a center, but he has also played right wing as well, which is his natural position. Backes had a career year in 2010–11 when he led the Blues in goals scored (31) and points (62). He was also plus 32 on the year, which was the best mark of any forward in the NHL, and 26 of his goals were scored five-on-five. These last two statistics show that Backes can not only produce offense, but that he can also shut down the best the opposition has to offer.

Part of what makes Backes most effective is how he uses his size. With it, he is a handful in front of the net and is difficult to stop on a charging rush. When he gets the puck, he has a hard, accurate wrist shot, and he also has great eye-hand coordination that allows him to tip drives in from the point. The Blues have a few defensemen that can deliver a strong drive on net, but Backes is more than willing to stand in those dangerous spots if it means scoring a goal.

The Blues obviously noticed the drive and leadership exhibited by Backes, and they named him captain for the 2011–12 season. This campaign saw Backes score a little less (24 goals and 54 points) than the season before, but he was still a top point producer on the club.

St. Louis is a good enough team to be a yearly Cup contender, and they were back in the playoffs for the

The term "power forward" is used in hockey to describe a strong, large-bodied player who uses his size and strength to go to the net, create chaos and score goals. Too often, though, the term is inappropriately used to describe forwards who have the correct physical dimensions but do not play the robust game of a power forward. Such is not the case for St. Louis Blues winger David Backes, who, in fact, seems to be the embodiment of the term. The 6-foot-3, 225-pound Backes plays a physical, punishing game, and, for good measure, he can score goals too. But, best of all, he puts his heart and soul into every game he plays.

A native of Blaine, Minnesota, Backes attended Spring Lake Park High School where he scored 46 goals and recorded 112 points in 48 career games between 1999

first time in three years after finishing as the second best team in the Western Conference in 2011–12. The Blues defeated the San Jose Sharks in five games during the opening round, but the Los Angeles Kings upset them in the second round. St. Louis' undoing in the playoffs was because of the team's lack of offense, which is something the club will need to address if it hopes to advance further in the postseason. New coach Ken Hitchcock's defense-first attitude greatly helped the underachieving Blues succeed, but players like Backes, T.J. Oshie, David Perron, Alex Steen, Chris Stewart, Patrik Berglund and Alex Pietrangelo are going to need to find more offense within the system. It should, however, for the foreseeable future, be a comfort to these players that they will continue to be backed up by the solid goaltending duo of Jaroslav Halak and Brian Elliot.

> Drafted 62nd overall by the St. Louis Blues in 2003

> Twice scored 31 goals in a season

> Named captain of the Blues in 2011

> Recorded over 90 penalty minutes five consecutive seasons

> Recorded 126 goals and 272 points in 446 career games

CAREER HIGHLIGHTS

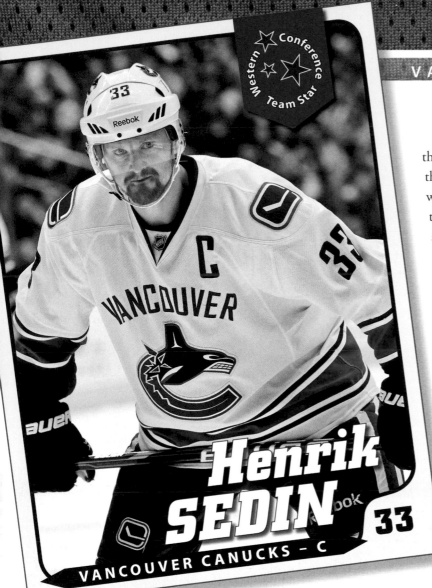

Western Conference Team Star

Henrik SEDIN 33
VANCOUVER CANUCKS – C

Sedin also won the Art Ross Trophy at the end of the 2009–10 season with a league-best 112 points. At that point, no other member of the Canucks had ever won the award, though many had come close. Former team captain Markus Naslund finished second in scoring on two occasions (2001–01 and 2002–03) and former stars like Pavel Bure, Alex Mogilny and Todd Bertuzzi all challenged for the award at various points in their careers. Sedin, however, pulled off the feat with only 29 of his 112 points being goals, and those 29 goals were a career high.

Sedin's Art Ross Trophy campaign was not only the best in the NHL in 2009–10, it was the best point-producing regular season a Vancouver Canucks player has ever enjoyed, and for his efforts that year Sedin received the ultimate recognition from the NHL by being named the winner of the Hart Memorial Trophy as league MVP (which made him, once again, the first Canuck to win the award).

Vancouver fans have certainly appreciated Sedin's performances during the regular season, but they had to wait a long time before they could see how the Canucks and Sedin responded to playoff pressure. Vancouver finally broke through in the 2011 playoffs and made it all the way to Game 7 of the Stanley Cup final before losing to the Boston Bruins. It was not the finish Vancouver fans wanted, but it was proof that the Canucks were serious NHL contenders. As for Sedin, he had a solid postseason, contributing 19 assists and 3 goals in 25 games, but many hockey fans will only recall that the Canucks were badly mauled by the Bruins in three games played in Boston and that Sedin, as team captain, took the brunt of the criticism. The numbers, however, speak for themselves, and Sedin finished the 2011–12 regular season tied for seventh place in league scoring, with close to a point-per-game pace as he collected 81 points in 82 games played.

It's interesting to note that Sedin was the only player from the Western Conference to be in the top 10

H enrik Sedin is simply one of the best passers in the history of the NHL. Case in point: the 6-foot-2, 188-pound Vancouver Canucks center has played in 892 career games, registered 576 assists and led the league in assists for the past three seasons with 83, 75 and 67, respectively. Sedin always shows a knack for going on the attack and finding the holes in the opposition's defense; he can also make a pass from anywhere on the ice, and, on occasion, will take a shot that finds its way into the back of the net. Further, since Sedin came into the league with his identical twin brother Daniel, the on-ice chemistry between them has been magic to watch. Of the two, Henrik is the playmaker, and he routinely puts the puck on the stick of his more goal-oriented brother.

(finishing 9th) of all 2011–12 point producers (Ray Whitney of the Phoenix Coyotes had the next best point total from the West with 77 points to finish 13th). Sedin explains these numbers with his opinion that the different style of play between the East and West is the reason why there are so few players from the Western Conference among the league leaders in points.

In light of 2010–11's postseason success, Canucks fans were hopeful of a return trip to the finals in the 2012 postseason, but the eighth-place Los Angeles Kings had other plans and took their first-round series in five games. During this series, Daniel Sedin was recovering from a concussion and only played two games, but Henrik still managed to record five points and demonstrate on more than one occasion that he can still be productive, even if his brother is not playing.

Sedin is likely to be a steady point producer for the next few years. Nevertheless, Vancouver fans would likely appreciate a grittier Sedin who scores more goals in order to get the team over the top to capture the elusive Stanley Cup, which would, of course, be another Vancouver first.

MASKED
MARVELS

Roberto
LUONGO
VANCOUVER CANUCKS - G
1

Pekka
RINNE
NASHVILLE PREDATORS - G
35

Henrik
LUNDQVIST
NEW YORK RANGERS - G
30

Mike
SMITH

Miikka
KIPRUSOFF
CALGARY FLAMES – G

Martin
BRODEUR
NEW JERSEY DEVILS

Jaroslav
HALAK
ST. LOUIS BLUES – G
41

Marc-Andre
FLEURY
PITTSBURGH PENGUINS – G
29

Jimmy
HOWARD
DETROIT RED WINGS – G

Jonathan
QUICK
LOS ANGELES KINGS – G
32

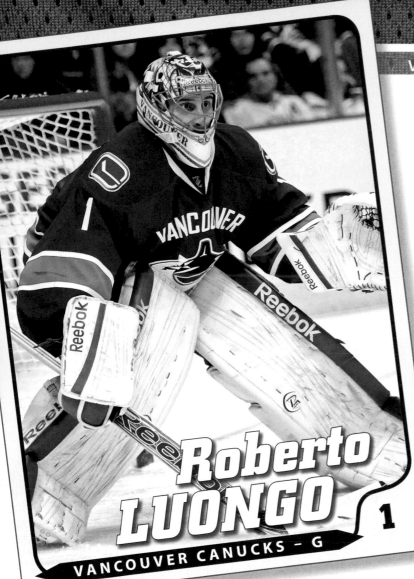

Roberto
LUONGO

VANCOUVER CANUCKS – G

1

to have his chance in net.

Back in the fall of 2006, Canucks fans were thrilled to finally have a quality goalie like Luongo. At the time, the club had pulled off a rather lopsided trade with the Florida Panthers that sent disgraced forward Todd Bertuzzi, stay-at-home defenseman Bryan Allen and backup goalie Alex Auld south and Luongo north. Since then, all the 6-foot-3, 208-pound Luongo has done is post stellar seasons. In his six years on the West Coast he has achieved season-win totals of 47, 35, 33, 40, 38 and 31, he has led the team to two Presidents' Trophy wins and he has come within one game of winning the Stanley Cup. Despite this glowing résumé (along with an Olympic gold-medal-win in 2010, which was won in Vancouver), Luongo has become the scapegoat for the franchise's inability to win the Cup.

Luongo has always been serious about playing hockey and being a top-notch goaltender. He started out as a dedicated ball-hockey player who loved to strap on the pads and pretend to be goaltending legend and Hall of Famer Grant Fuhr. Originally, the Quebec native was actually discouraged from playing in net by his mother, but she soon realized that Luongo was determined to stop pucks. He was 11 years old when he finally got his chance on the ice and he quickly recorded his first shutout.

Fast-forward several years and Luongo now gets his fair share of NHL shutouts, notching his 60th in 2011–12. His career numbers are also strong, with 339 wins, a .919 save percentage and a 2.52 goals-against average. True, he is a legendarily slow starter and he has a propensity for streakiness, but he is a strong student of the game. He rarely gets rattled and is known for being a cool character. Additionally, when Luongo is playing well, he uses his large size to great advantage and displays a terrific catching hand. Simply put, he is a competitive player who doesn't like to be beaten, even in practice.

T he 2012 Stanley Cup playoffs were supposed to give Vancouver Canucks goalie Roberto Luongo what many saw as a last chance at glory. It didn't happen, even though he had nearly pulled it off a year earlier when he took the Canucks all the way to the seventh game of the final only to lose on home ice by a score of 4–0. It was a loss not taken well in Vancouver (hockey fans will recall the riots in the streets afterward), and Luongo looked forward to a chance at redemption in 2012. The Los Angeles Kings, however, had other ideas in mind, and they knocked off the Canucks in just five playoff games. In fact, Luongo didn't even play in the last three of those five games. He had lost each of the first two matches by a score of 4–2, and it seemed as if everyone was pulling for backup Cory Schneider

Until the Canucks reached the Stanley Cup final in 2011, it was commonly said that Luongo couldn't steal playoff games for his team. However, after series wins over the Nashville Predators, San Jose Sharks and archrival Chicago Blackhawks, that claim started to lose its weight. Luongo recorded two shutouts in the final versus the Boston Bruins (1–0 in both the opener and in the fifth game), but the last win proved elusive, which fueled the talk that Luongo couldn't win big games. The series went to a hard-fought seven games, but Luongo received little in the way of on-ice support from his teammates, and he certainly didn't garner any sympathy from the unforgiving Canucks fans.

Luongo has made it clear he will consider waiving his no-trade rights so that the Canucks will have options in light of the fact that Schneider is now ready to be a top goalie in the league. This might seem like the right thing for Luongo to do at this stage in his career, but it is just as likely that the Vancouver Canucks and their fans will end up appreciating Luongo much more once he is wearing another uniform.

> Drafted 4th overall by the New York Islanders in 1997

> Two-time NHL Second Team All-Star

> Led the NHL in wins in 2010–11 with 38

> Member of Canadian gold-medal-winning team at the 2010 Winter Olympics

> Posted a 339–283–83 record with 60 shutouts in 727 career games

CAREER HIGHLIGHTS

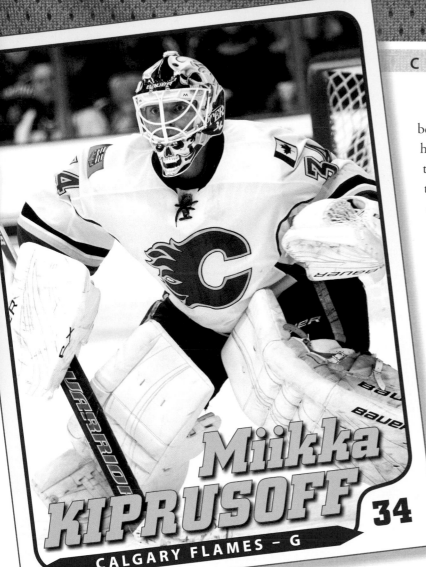

Miikka
KIPRUSOFF
34
CALGARY FLAMES – G

because of how Kiprusoff used his legs. The move, however, was actually an innovative desperation-play the acrobatic goaltender had used before. Nevertheless, the save was nearly impossible and the Flames went on to win the match, with Kiprusoff making a total of 34 saves on the night, all of which helped him to become the 27th NHL goalie to reach the 300-career-win plateau.

It was only fitting that the 6-foot-1, 184-pound Finland-born netminder recorded the milestone in San Jose. The Sharks had originally selected Kiprusoff 116th overall in the 1995 NHL entry draft, and he was still deep on their depth chart when the Flames started to snoop around for a goalie in November 2003. At the beginning of their hunt, the Flames wanted Vesa Toskala, who was backing up Sharks starter Evgeni Nabokov. The Sharks turned down the opportunity to move Toskala and instead offered up Kiprusoff in exchange for a 2005 second-round draft choice. The Flames ended up winning the trade, and, in essence, stole away one of the best goalies in hockey for a mere draft pick.

The Sharks have probably kicked themselves a few times for letting such a strong presence in net go to a conference rival. They were likely especially irked when Kiprusoff helped to eliminate San Jose in the 2004 postseason, after which they had to watch as the Flames took the Tampa Bay Lightning to seven games before ultimately losing the Stanley Cup. The Sharks have never made it this far and thoughts inevitably turn to "what if?" had the team hung on to Kiprusoff when it had the chance.

Since his arrival in Calgary, Kiprusoff has been remarkable. With the Sharks, he had played in just 47 games over three seasons, but since the trade in 2003, he has rarely been out of the Flames' net. He posted a 24–10–4 record to complete the 2003–04 campaign, and then won 15 games in the playoffs before losing the last showdown 2–1. Since then, Kiprusoff has played in at least 70 regular-season games per year, and despite his

L ate in 2009 in a one-goal game against the San Jose Sharks, Calgary Flames goalie Miikka Kiprusoff preserved his club's lead when he made what many called the "save of the year." Sharks defenseman Brent Burns let a drive go from the point and Kiprusoff literally went flat-out to stop it. With Kiprusoff seemingly down for the count, San Jose forward Joe Pavelski swatted at the rebound. His attempt was on its way over and behind Kiprusoff when, at the last second, the Flames' netminder threw up his legs in a scissor-like motion and trapped the puck between his pads. Sharks forwards Joe Thornton and Patrick Marleau were left with nothing as Kiprusoff was able to hold on to the puck until the whistle was blown. Afterward, the game's TV announcers called the save "the scorpion"

above-average games-played total, his save percentage has never dipped below the .906 mark. Kiprusoff was also a First Team All-Star in 2005–06 and took home the Vezina Trophy that same season.

Over the past seven seasons, Kiprusoff has won at least 35 games per season as well as posted 40-plus wins on three occasions, with an impressive personal record of 45 in 2008–09. Beyond that, it was early in the 2011–12 season when he broke Mike Vernon's franchise record for most career wins by a Flames goaltender. The win was his 263rd, and by the end of the season he had won 297 games.

The tremendous workload the Flames put on Kiprusoff only seems to make him better, but it would be interesting to see how he would respond if the number of games he played was reduced to a range of 60 to 65. Popular thought suggests he would likely be tougher to beat, but the reduced playing time will probably never happen because the Flames are afraid to go without their star in any important game — and it's not difficult to

understand why. Simply put, without Kiprusoff's heroics on an almost nightly basis, the current Flames would not factor into many conversations about playoff contention.

Kiprusoff was rewarded with a six-year $35 million contract in 2008, and while rumors might sometimes swirl of thoughts of trading the man known as "Kipper," such notions are probably quickly discounted when the Flames recall the fact that they hope to make the playoffs sometime soon.

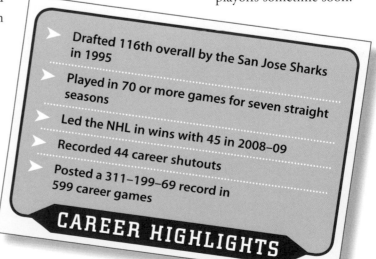

- ▶ Drafted 116th overall by the San Jose Sharks in 1995
- ▶ Played in 70 or more games for seven straight seasons
- ▶ Led the NHL in wins with 45 in 2008–09
- ▶ Recorded 44 career shutouts
- ▶ Posted a 311–199–69 record in 599 career games

CAREER HIGHLIGHTS

Henrik LUNDQVIST 30

NEW YORK RANGERS - G

New York Rangers goaltender Henrik Lundqvist has done something no other goalie in the National Hockey League has done before — he has won 30+ games in the first seven seasons of his career. During those seven years Lundqvist has slowly but surely climbed to the top of his position and few if any other netminder in the league can challenge his domination. If anyone needs proof of that assertion, just look at his Vezina-winning performance during the 2011–12 season. Lundqvist won 39 games (a career high for the Swedish-born goalie), posted a .930 save percentage (his best mark to date), recorded a goals-against average of 1.97 and for good measure he tossed in eight shutouts to bring his career total to 43 (putting him just six shy of Eddie Giacomin's franchise record

of 49). Under the abrasive leadership of coach John Tortorella the Rangers finished first in the Eastern Conference with a remarkable 51–24–7 record and 109 points for the 2011–12 campaign. But make no mistake, it would all have fallen apart without the 6-foot-1, 205-pound Lundqvist playing superbly during his 62 appearances over the season.

Lundqvist is an incredibly quick and agile goalie, and that allows him to play deep in his net. A typical goalie comes out away from the net and toward the puck, to cut down the shooter's angle and give them less space to shoot at. Lundqvist relies on his reflexes to help him cover holes normally covered by goalies who play the angle. What Lundqvist gains by playing so deep in his crease is the ability to never be out of position. He can square up to shooters wherever they may be, and he can move quickly from post to post on cross-crease attempts, backdoor plays and wraparounds. The collapsing style of defense that the Rangers play is tailored to Lundqvist's style. By stacking people in front of the net the way the Rangers do, it is difficult for the opposition to get clean shots through and pick the corners that Lundqvist's style leaves open. Also, with the Rangers' defense playing so close to the goalie, they can easily clear any rebounds that Lundqvist may leave.

The city of New York loves a star, and the fans at Madison Square Garden have certainly taken to Lundqvist, often chanting "Hen-rik, Hen-rik" as he stars in game after game. When he first became a Ranger he was forced to adhere to a team rule that all first year players cannot live in the city. Lundqvist and his wife are now living in Manhattan and enjoy all the benefits the city has to offer. The sharply dressed, handsome goalie loves the area and the people and he stays there most of the year. All things considered it would be difficult to see Lundqvist playing or residing anywhere else.

There is one more hurdle for Lundqvist to jump — getting the Rangers back to the Stanley Cup final for the

first time since 1994. It nearly happened in 2012 but the Rangers ran out of steam when they played the New Jersey Devils in the conference final. It was said that Martin Brodeur of the Devils outdueled Lundqvist, but that is an unfair assessment. The fact is that the Rangers needed goal scoring, and the hope is that the offseason signing of sniper Rick Nash will help fill the void.

The 29-year-old Lundqvist is not only the most valuable player on the New York Rangers team, he is quite possibly the MVP of the entire league. No team relies on their goalie quite like the Rangers do Lundqvist, and they have done so since he first entered the league in the 2005–06 season. Lundqvist played 53 games as rookie and won 30 of them, and he has never looked back. He has played 70-plus games five times, and the Rangers would be wise to keep that number somewhere between 60 and 65 if they want to win a Stanley Cup with Lundqvist in goal. In 2010–11 Lundqvist's 11 shutouts were the most in

any season for a Ranger netminder since John Ross Roach had 13 in 1928–29.

If Lundqvist can continue his Vezina-winning ways, and the Rangers can get their trio of top-flight forwards — Rick Nash, Brad Richards and Marian Gaborik — going, the Broadway Blueshirts look to be in fine form.

► Drafted 205th overall by the New York Rangers in 2000

► Named winner of the Vezina Trophy in 2012

► Named to the NHL's First All-Star Team in 2012

► Recorded 30 or more wins in all seven NHL seasons

► Posted a 252–155–54 record in 468 career games

CAREER HIGHLIGHTS

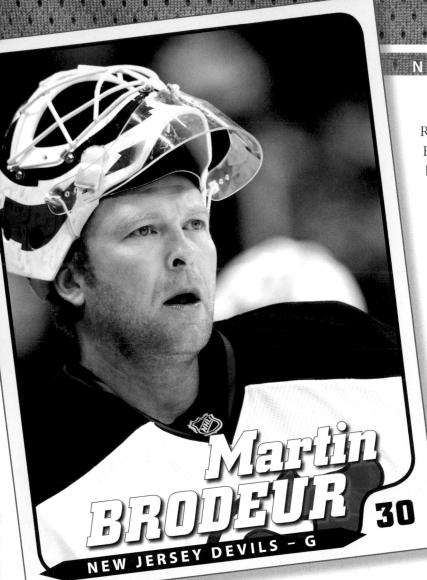

Martin BRODEUR 30

NEW JERSEY DEVILS – G

On the night of May 8, 2012, goaltender Martin Brodeur, who had just turned 40 two days earlier, took the New Jersey Devils past the Philadelphia Flyers with a 3–1 victory in Game 6 of their playoff series. The Devils then proceeded to knock off the New York Rangers to gain a spot in the Stanley Cup final for the first time in 11 years. It would have been the perfect ending for Brodeur to win his fourth Cup and then retire, but the Los Angeles Kings had other ideas and subdued the Devils in six games. Brodeur did everything he could to keep his team in contention against the Kings, but the opposition was too deep. Despite the loss, Brodeur posted a record of 14–9 in the 2012 playoffs, which brought his career playoff mark to 113 wins, a number second only to Patrick

Roy's 151 postseason victories. In fact, as far as Brodeur's stats are concerned, this might end up being one of the few records Roy will still hold over Brodeur once the Devils goalie retires.

Brodeur was drafted 20th overall by the Devils in 1990 and played his first full season in 1993–94. Since then, he has set just about every important NHL goaltending record. The marks include most regular season wins (656), most career shutouts (119), most games played (1,191), most minutes played (70,029), and most career playoff shutouts (24). Brodeur is also the only goalie to eight times record 40 or more wins in a season. His career goals-against average is a mere 2.23 and his save percentage sits at a remarkable .913. In short, there is nothing left for Brodeur to prove and he can only add to his legacy for however long he decides to stay in the game. Truly, the only substantial mark he could aim to achieve would be to add one last Stanley Cup ring to his collection, a feat that would put him into the same company as Roy and Terry Sawchuk, who are the two legendary NHL netminders Brodeur has been most often compared to throughout his illustrious career.

Brodeur has been fortunate to enjoy good health over most of his career. The only time he suffered a major injury was during the 2008–09 season when his elbow was damaged, which restricted his appearances to just 31. He still, however, managed to go 19–9–3 in that campaign, and in 2011–12, he played in 59 games and won 31 times which helped the Devils get back to the playoffs after they missed out the previous season. The team always turns to Brodeur when it needs to win or go on a long run in the playoffs, but at his age, Brodeur cannot focus on being the dominating 70-plus game goaltender as he once was. Rather, he must use his experience and knowledge to be a big-game goaltender and win when it matters most.

Brodeur has never played any style but his own and he has stayed away from the modern goaltending gurus.

The unflappable goalie consistently plays with the old stand-up method, hitting the ice only when he has to. He has admittedly modified his technique to suit the new realities of the NHL, which is a different game than when he first started in the early 1990s, but his ability to handle and pass the puck is still the best of any goaltender in the league and it is always clear that the athletic Brodeur loves to compete. He has been the Devils' No. 1 netminder for 18 consecutive seasons and has taken his team to the Stanley Cup final a total of five times. He almost always shows a cool disposition and usually has a huge smile on his face.

It is unknown how much longer Brodeur will play in the NHL, but he is still effective enough to hold his status in the league as a top netminder. It's inevitable, of course, that the Devils will eventually have to replace their future Hall of Fame goalie, but they understandably want to hold off on that for just a little longer, having signed him to a two-year extension after the Stanley Cup final. Hockey fans also hope for the same longevity because greatness of Brodeur's caliber is too often missing from the modern game played in today's NHL.

> Drafted 20th overall by the New Jersey Devils in 1990

> Won 40 or more games in a season eight times

> Four-time winner of the Vezina Trophy

> Named to the NHL's First All-Star Team four times

> Posted a 656–371–141 record in 1,191 career games

CAREER HIGHLIGHTS

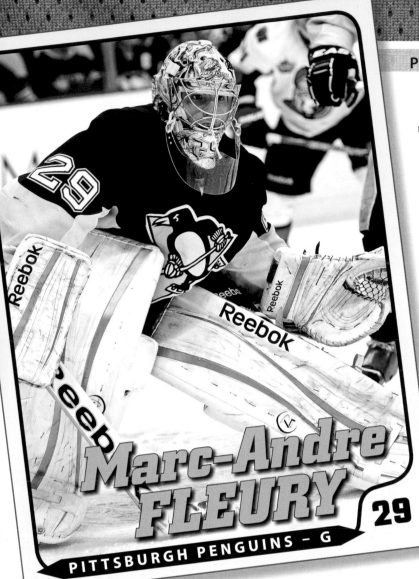

Marc-Andre FLEURY

PITTSBURGH PENGUINS – G **29**

them, they were on the outside looking in after being ousted in six games.

The total team collapse that saw the Penguins exit the 2012 playoffs earlier than many expected had many components, and Fleury's performance in net was definitely one of them. The normally dependable goalie allowed 26 goals against over the six-game series for a goals-against average of 4.63. The good news for Pittsburgh is that Fleury has bounced back from adversity many times in his career. When he started with the Penguins in 2003–04, the team was in the middle of a rebuilding phase and was one of the weaker teams in the league. Fleury played in 21 games that season, going 4–14–2. Then, at Christmastime, the 20-year-old Fleury was released by the Penguins to play for Canada at the World Junior Championships. He had a strong tournament, going 4–1 with a 1.81 goals-against average, but his defining moment of the World Juniors happened late in the gold-medal game when he put a goal into his own net by hitting a Canadian defenseman with a clearing attempt. Canada lost and took home the silver medal, and Fleury was sent back to his Quebec Major Junior Hockey League club in Cape Breton to finish out the season. He then spent 2004–05 with the Penguins' American Hockey League farm team in Wilkes-Barre, Pennsylvania, where he proved he could bounce back as he posted a 26–19–4 record, a 2.52 goals-against average and a .901 save percentage in the year the NHL was shut down for the season.

He became the Penguins' regular netminder in 2005–06 when he played in 50 games. Still, it was a mental struggle for Fleury, as he only won 13 times for the rebuilding team. He won 40 contests in 2006–07, but injuries held his next season to just 35 appearances. The Penguins, however, made it all the way to the finals during the 2008 playoffs and Fleury posted his career-best playoff numbers with a 1.97 goals-against average and a .933 save percentage. Still, when it mattered

Goaltender Marc-Andre Fleury and the Pittsburgh Penguins suffered a meltdown of epic proportions during the 2012 playoffs. The Penguins' netminder had enjoyed one of his best regular seasons since joining the NHL in 2003–04, as he recorded a career-high 42 victories (the second most in the league) and posted a save percentage of .913 and a goals-against average of 2.36. In fact, Fleury's good play was one of the main reasons the injury-riddled Penguins made the playoffs in the Eastern Conference with a 51–26–6 record. Further, prior to the start of the playoffs, the Penguins were the odds-on favorite to represent the Eastern Conference in the Stanley Cup final, but a first-round matchup with the Philadelphia Flyers went horribly wrong and before the Penguins knew what hit most, he and the Penguins couldn't top the Detroit Red Wings and Pittsburgh lost the Cup in six games.

The Penguins vowed the results would be different in 2009, and they again made the Stanley Cup final, and again played against Detroit for the crown. The Penguins lost the first two games, but they bounced back and shut the door on Detroit as Fleury gave up just two goals over the final two games. He also made a heart-stopping save on Detroit defenseman Nicklas Lidstrom to close out the last game and give the Penguins their third championship. No goalie had won the Stanley Cup in Game 7 on the road since Ken Dryden did it for the Montreal Canadiens in 1971 when they beat the Chicago Blackhawks in their hometown.

Fleury, Sidney Crosby, Evgeni Malkin and Jordan Staal were all draft picks that were meant to lead the Penguins to success, but since their Cup win, Fleury and company have only been able to take the team past the first round

of the playoffs once in the last three seasons. And now, with the departure of Staal in the 2012 off-season and a blue line that needs improvement, the Penguins and their goalie will need to be even better if they want to repeat as Cup champions. Hopefully the newly signed Tomas Vokoun will give the Penguins a viable backup option in net to assist and provide Fleury some rest during the regular season and perhaps in the playoffs as well.

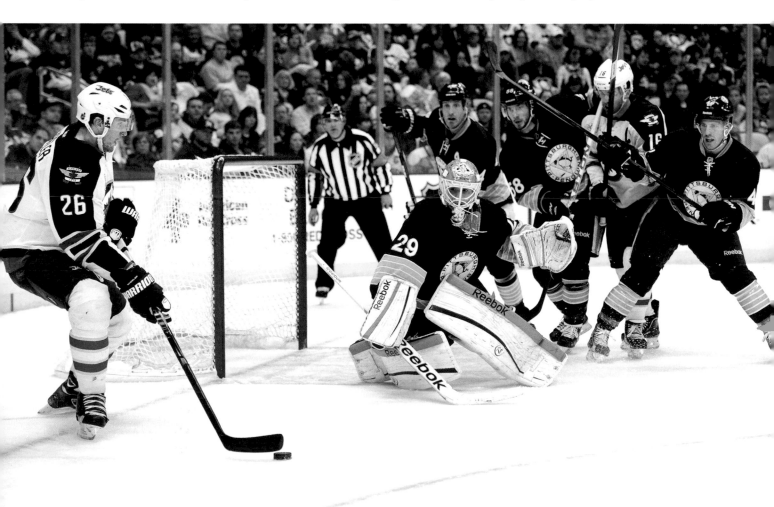

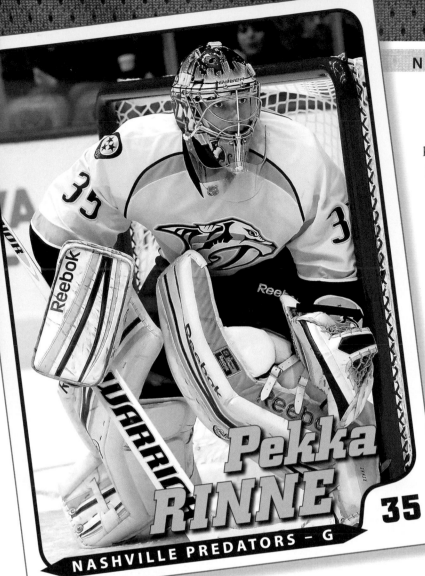

Pekka
RINNE

35

NASHVILLE PREDATORS – G

Before Rinne's arrival, the Predators were mired in postseason mediocrity. In each of Nashville's three playoff appearances post-2005 lockout, they were ousted in the first round despite having excellent regular-season records. Neither Tomas Vokoun nor Chris Mason had fared well between the pipes, and while Dan Ellis was better, his performance wasn't exactly worth a standing ovation. So, after spending two seasons with the American Hockey League's Milwaukee Admirals, Rinne made his NHL debut in 2008–09, eventually usurping Ellis. Rinne immediately recorded three shutouts, becoming the first rookie goalie to accomplish the feat since Martin Biron did the same nearly nine years earlier.

The following season, Rinne posted his first season of at least 30 wins (32 total), which meant he joined Vokoun as only the second goalie in franchise history to reach the milestone. The Predators as a whole, however, didn't fare so well in the playoffs that year and were out after six games with the eventual Cup-winning Chicago Blackhawks.

The 2010–11 season brought better times, as it was a breakthrough year for both Rinne and the Predators franchise. Longtime coach Barry Trotz instilled a solid defensive system and Nashville stifled their opposition en route to posting the league's third-best goals-against average. Rinne's numbers were outstanding. His save percentage was .930, second-best in the league, and he ranked third in goals-against average, with 2.12. Still, the best was yet to come for Nashville. In April 2011, fans filled Bridgestone Arena to watch the Predators end their playoff curse — they defeated the Anaheim Ducks for Nashville's first series win in franchise history. The Predators were eliminated by the Vancouver Canucks in the following round, but Rinne had a phenomenal series against Vancouver that saw him finish with a goals-against average of 1.94 and a save percentage of .932. For his efforts, he was named to the NHL's Second All-Star Team at the end of the season and was

Scouts who can unearth late-round gems in the NHL entry draft are worth their weight in gold, and Janne Kekalainen is one such example. He was the scout who suggested the Nashville Predators think about taking goaltender Pekka Rinne. On Kekalainen's advice, then–assistant general manager Ray Shero went to Finland in 2004 to get a closer look at the netminder while he was serving as the backup to Niklas Backstrom, who was also destined for a future in the NHL. Shero had the chance to see Rinne in the pre-game warmup, and Kekalainen had only seen Rinne start two games, but it was enough for the Predators to take a flyer on the 6-foot-5, 209-pound goaltender. He was chosen 258th in the 2004 draft, and no one associated with the selection of Rinne has ever regretted it.

runner-up to the Boston Bruins' Tim Thomas for the Vezina Trophy.

In November 2011, Nashville general manager David Poile rewarded Rinne by signing him to a seven-year, $49 million contract extension. Rinne continued his excellent play in 2011–12, leading the NHL with 43 wins and earning a second Vezina Trophy nomination. Rinne was a workhorse in the Predators net, with 73 appearances and a second-place finish in minutes played (4,168). His league-leading 1,987 saves were also a testament to his status as the last line of defense.

Rinne has perhaps the best catching hand in the entire NHL, and he loves to snatch the puck in his glove every chance he gets. He grew up in Finland playing a game similar to baseball, and it was this sport that helped to develop his great glove hand. Rinne uses his lanky body in an acrobatic fashion to stop the shots he doesn't catch, and his excellent play covers for many of the Predators' problems.

The limitations, however, of a small hockey

market such as Nashville are seen in the Predators' salary-cap constraints. Poile's commitment to Rinne may force valuable players to leave the team, but while there may be question marks throughout the Predators roster, there's no doubt that Rinne is Nashville's foundation in goal.

- Drafted 258th overall by the Nashville Predators in 2004
- Won an NHL-best 43 games in 2011–12
- Named to the NHL's Second All-Star Team in 2011
- Recorded 25 career shutouts
- Posted a 138–72–26 record in 250 career games

CAREER HIGHLIGHTS

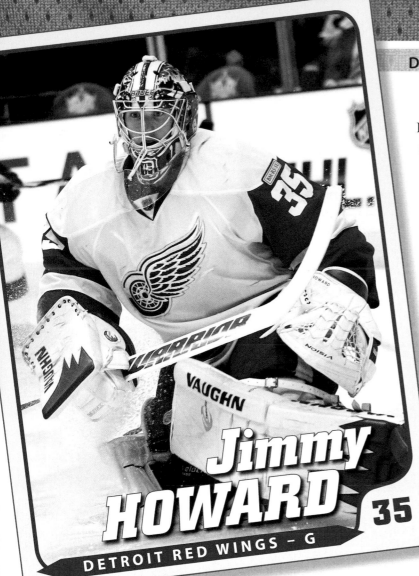

Jimmy
HOWARD 35
DETROIT RED WINGS – G

Howard cut his teeth, patrolling the Griffins' crease for four full seasons. Over that time he went 90–73–11, with occasional call-ups to the Red Wings bench. Howard played nine NHL games between 2005–06 and 2008–09 (winning one game), and during the 2008 playoffs he was with the team when they won the Stanley Cup, which gave him a chance to observe veteran goalie Chris Osgood as he backstopped the team to another championship. It was a great learning experience for Howard, who had the opportunity to see what it took to win it all.

As Howard was developing his game in the minors, the Red Wings did a smart thing by bringing in a group of veteran netminders. Manny Legace, Joey MacDonald, Dominik Hasek and Ty Conklin joined Osgood in manning the Detroit net until Howard got promoted for the 2009–10 season, which was a year that saw Howard finish second in rookie-of-the-year voting for the Calder Memorial Trophy (he lost out to Buffalo Sabres defenseman Tyler Myers). His 37 wins and .924 save percentage in his first NHL season had firmly established Howard as a legitimate NHL player, and his coming-out party was topped at the end of the season with a nomination to the All-Rookie Team.

Howard, listed at 6-feet-tall and 210 pounds, tends to play smaller than his size, thriving on his athleticism, quick reflexes and positioning. He is, however, susceptible to bad rebounds, but as he gains maturity his control should improve. Above all, though, Howard is extremely competitive, which is a positive trait for any hockey player, but particularly so for a goaltender.

Since Howard became Detroit's starter, he has won 37, 37 and 35 games, respectively, over three seasons, which has put him in the top tier of NHL puckstoppers. Howard has always had a save percentage above .900 and his career goals-against average is 2.41. Unfortunately, though, he has yet to lead Detroit deep into the playoffs, and in goaltending, all the regular-season success in the world can go out the window if the

Third-year NHL goalie Jimmy Howard is working his way toward becoming an elite puckstopper for the Detroit Red Wings. The team selected Howard 64th overall in the 2003 NHL entry draft after management decided they liked how the college program at the University of Maine had developed Howard. His 47–23–10 record in 87 career games didn't hurt either, and in order to develop those skills for the NHL, Detroit general manager Ken Holland, once a professional goalie himself, was determined not to rush the native of Syracuse, New York, into the big league. Howard needed to work at building up his mind and body to survive a much longer NHL regular season, so he was assigned to play with the Grand Rapids Griffins of the American Hockey League. It was there that puck can't be stopped when it matters most.

The playoffs have been a bit of a roller-coaster ride for Howard, and the pressure of playing for Detroit in the postseason is becoming a continuing saga. In his first playoff year, Howard helped Detroit eliminate the Phoenix Coyotes in the first round, but was out after just five games when the San Jose Sharks met the Red Wings in the next series. Virtually the same thing happened in the 2010–11 postseason, albeit the second-round loss to the Sharks featured Detroit coming back from a 3–0 deficit to force a seventh game. Another year later, in the 2011–12 playoffs, Detroit played in a short series against the Nashville Predators, who won in five games. Howard's playoff record now stands at a mediocre 13–15.

Howard has heard from the demanding Detroit fans about his playoff performances, but he under- stands that long-term results will ultimately tell the story of his playoff career. Detroit is an older squad and a perennial Stanley Cup threat, and after 21 consecutive years of making the playoffs, Detroit and Howard are hopeful for a few more playoff chances yet.

- Drafted 64th overall by the Detroit Red Wings in 2003
- Posted a 90–73–11 career record for Grand Rapids Griffins (AHL)
- Named to the NHL's All-Rookie Team in 2010
- Won 35 or more games in each of his first three NHL seasons
- Posted a 110–54–19 record in 192 career games

CAREER HIGHLIGHTS

Jonathan QUICK
32
LOS ANGELES KINGS – G

When goaltender Jonathan Quick was eight years old and growing up in Hamden, Connecticut, he watched as the New York Rangers won their first Stanley Cup in 54 years. The year was 1994 and an American-born goalie Mike Richter led the Rangers to the championship. Richter became a hero to the youngster and Quick liked to recall a particular save the New York netminder made on Pavel Bure of the Vancouver Canucks in the 1994 final. Little did Quick know that 18 years later he would take the Los Angeles Kings to their first ever Stanley Cup title, ending a 45 year drought.

Quick was a talented athlete as a youngster and excelled at baseball and football, but hockey was his first love from the time he was just five years of age.

Being involved in so many sports meant there was overlapping seasons and it came to the point where Quick had to decide which one sport he would pursue. Quick knew it was a hockey career he wanted to chase and his parents were dedicated to finding the best competition available for their budding goalie. By the time he was 12 years old, hockey people were telling the Quick family that Jonathan had NHL potential.

Quick played high school hockey for Avon Old Farms boys' school, which had always been known for its excellent hockey program. He got off to a bit of a slow start in his first year when he was 17 years old, but the next two years saw him raise his win total to 53 in 61 games. During the 2004–05 season he posted a record of 25–2 and that got the attention of the Los Angeles Kings who selected the 6-foot-1, 212-pound Quick with the 72nd pick of the 2005 entry draft. The Kings kept a close eye on their new prospect after he left high school and enrolled in college for a couple of seasons. From there he was assigned to the Manchester Monarchs of the American Hockey League, but he also had to spend time with the Reading royals of the lower-level East Coast Hockey League. He always posted winning records, but his play in the AHL was not outstanding. However, injuries to other King netminders gave Quick a chance to play in the big league, and he has never looked back.

Quick had played in three games for the Kings in the 2007–08 season (winning twice) but got into 44 games (recording 21–18–2) just one year later. Over the next two seasons with Los Angeles, Quick won a total of 74 games and showed he deserved to be the number one goalie. He managed to achieve this even though the Kings had taken another goalie (Jonathan Bernier) with a high pick in the 2006 draft. Quick did not let the competition worry him at all; he was now a much more mature and focused player. As good as he was during the regular season, Quick was not nearly so effective in the playoffs, and the Kings were out in the first round in both the 2010 and 2011 playoffs. Quick would falter and tire in the post-season but he was gaining valuable experience.

The 2011–12 season was clearly Quick's best in the NHL to date. He carried a low scoring team (the Kings only scored 194 goals during the season — the second worst mark in the entire league) to a playoff spot by registering 35 wins and 13 ties. In many games the Kings did not even score two goals, yet Quick led the league in shutouts with 10 and posted a goals-against average of just 1.95. It was more of the same in the playoffs when he won 16 games and suffered only four defeats. The Kings lost just one road game, and his goals-against average actually went down to 1.41. It was

a dominating performance by Quick and he was justly rewarded with the Conn Smythe Trophy as the best player in the 2012 playoffs.

After a slow climb to the top, Quick is now king of the road as far as NHL goaltenders are concerned — and is inspiring his own generation of American youth goalies.

Jaroslav
HALAK

41

ST. LOUIS BLUES – G

for both goalies were remarkably similar and remarkably good. Halak went 26–12–7 in 46 games played and had a 1.97 goals-against average and a .926 save percentage. Elliott played in 38 games and posted a record of 23–10–4 with a 1.56 goals-against average and a .940 save percentage. It was a great situation for the Blues to be in and they won 49 games and recorded 109 points, second only to the Vancouver Canucks in the Western Conference.

The Blues were considered to be a playoff favorite prior to the start of the 2012 postseason, and they decided to go with Halak in the opening series against the San Jose Sharks. San Jose won Game 1, 3–2 in overtime, but St. Louis eventually took the series 4–1. However, in the next round against the Los Angeles Kings, with Elliott in net (due to an injury to Halak), the Blues got steamrolled by the Kings, losing in four straight games. Elliott was beaten for 15 goals in the four contests versus Los Angeles, and his poor performance put the spotlight back on Halak, who has had some measure of success in the postseason.

The Montreal Canadiens drafted the unknown Halak with the 271st selection in the 2003 entry draft, and while he was always good with the Habs, his best year in Montreal came in the 2009–10 season when he played in 45 games and posted a 26–13–5 record. He was also prominent that year for leading a rather average Canadiens squad to a pair of upsets over the Washington Capitals and Pittsburgh Penguins in the 2010 playoffs. Halak's great play kept Montreal favorite Carey Price on the bench throughout the playoffs, but as soon as the postseason was over, the Habs made it clear Price was going to be the man of the future and promptly dealt Halak to the Blues.

Halak's first season in St. Louis was not as good as everyone hoped it would be, even though he managed a 27–21–7 record with seven shutouts in 2010–11. The team missed the playoffs and Elliott was brought in to give Halak an experienced backup to play behind him

T he St. Louis Blues were the exception to the rule in the NHL in 2011–12: instead of employing one marquee netminder who played the lion's share of games, they tag-teamed the position, using two stellar goalies to balance their 82-game load. Most NHL teams like to know who their top goaltender is and they like to ride that main netminder throughout most of the regular season and the playoffs, but when Ken Hitchcock took over as coach of the Blues in the 14th game of the schedule, he thought it was a good idea to have both of his goalies ready. This meant that neither Jaroslav Halak, the acknowledged No. 1 goalie going into the season, nor Brian Elliott, a free-agent signing, was going to sit for very long. The end of the season showed the wisdom of Hitchcock's ways: the numbers in 2011–12. As the season moved along and the Blues realized they were happy with their goaltending duo, they decided to trade the once promising Ben Bishop to the Ottawa Senators. Now, however, it is inevitable that either Halak or Elliott will eventually emerge as the Blues' lead goalie.

Halak has always shown that he is a mobile goalie who covers the net well despite his size (5-foot-11 and 185 pounds). His style is a mixture of stand-up and low-to-the-ice play, and while at times he tends to play a little deep in his net, when he stands up and challenges the shooter to make the first move, his strategy is effective and difficult to beat.

As long as Hitchcock is coaching the Blues, they will be a good defensive team, which is something that helps the goalies immensely. Halak has what it takes to be an undisputed No.1 netminder in the NHL, and while the Blues are happy with the goaltending tandem they have, it is refreshing to know that Halak can take charge if he is called on to play the bulk of the schedule.

> Drafted 271st overall by the Montreal Canadiens in 2003

> Traded to the St. Louis Blues in June 2010

> Won 26 or more games in each of his last three seasons

> Shared (with Brian Elliott) the 2012 William M. Jennings Trophy

> Posted a 109–67–21 record in 204 career games

CAREER HIGHLIGHTS

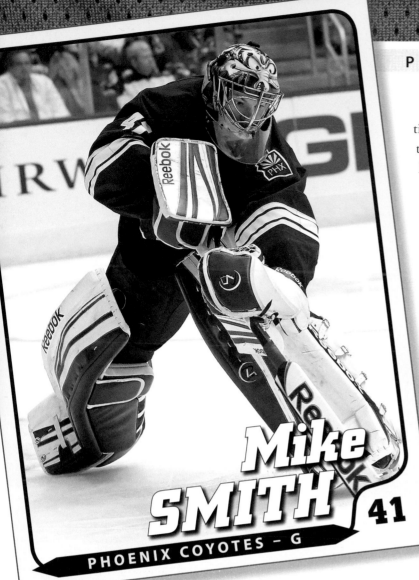

Mike SMITH **41**

PHOENIX COYOTES – G

In his teens, Mike Smith once attended a goaltending school in Mississauga, Ontario, and frankly he did not impress anyone with his ability to stop the puck. He had excellent size and showed excellent athletic prowess, but nobody watching him would have ever thought he was NHL-bound. Even Smith thought his career was over at one point, when the Tampa Bay Lightning placed him on waivers and no NHL team would take a chance on him despite a relatively inexpensive contract. However, the mentally tough Smith never gave up, and when the Phoenix Coyotes decided to take a chance on him he re-dedicated himself to the game he loves.

Smith excelled at softball when he was growing up in Kingston, Ontario, and won both provincial and national

titles at back catcher. Yet Smith soon came to believe that he had the athletic ability to become a goalie in hockey, but his minor career was hardly stellar. He was often a back-up netminder and when he made the Kingston Frontenacs of the Ontario Hockey League (OHL) in 1998–99, he played second fiddle to Andrew Raycroft, who famously was the Rookie of the Year for the 2003–04 NHL season before becoming a backup netminder himself. Things improved for Smith after a trade to the OHL's Sudbury Wolves during the 2000–01 season. He started the lion's share of games and posted a 22–13–7 record. It was the first time in his career that Smith was able to put all his skills together for a long stretch of consistent playing time. The Dallas Stars took a chance on the lanky 6-foot-4, 215-pound netminder and selected him 161st overall in the 2001 entry draft.

After he was drafted Smith took the long route to get to the NHL, playing for five different American Hockey League teams and one in the East Coast Hockey League between 2002 and 2006. He finally got a crack at an NHL job when he backed up Marty Turco in Dallas for the 2006–07 season. He showed well by going 12–5–2 for the Stars, and the next year saw him involved in a late season trade to the Tampa Bay Lightning.

What's more impressive is that Smith was so highly regarded by the Lightning that they traded him straight up for Brad Richards — a bona fide NHL star. Unfortunately, nothing seemed to go right for Smith in Tampa Bay and he would post a losing record in each of his first three seasons with the Lightning. In 2009–10, Smith posted a 13–6–1 record but he had long lost his starting job to veteran Dwayne Roloson. There appeared to be no room for Smith in Tampa Bay or in any other NHL city for that matter. He even spent time back in the minors playing for the Norfolk Admirals.

However the Coyotes liked what they saw of Smith when he was with Tampa and made the unrestricted free agent netminder a contract offer with one key

element — he was going to be the No.1 goalie in Phoenix. Smith signed and was eager to play for coach Dave Tippet, who knew him from his Dallas days. The move to Phoenix also promised work with longtime NHL goalie turned goalie coach Sean Burke.

Burke adjusted Smith's style and set him further back in his net so that he could react more quickly to cross-crease plays and tip attempts; he also worked at getting the now 30 year old goalie to mentally grasp that he was indeed a No.1 goalie, and to play with that confidence. It all worked out beautifully for Smith and the Coyotes. Smith had the best year of his life with 38 wins, a .930 save percentage and

eight shutouts during the regular season. In the playoffs he led Phoenix over Chicago and Nashville, despite his team being outshot almost every night.

The low scoring Coyotes could not produce enough offense to get past Los Angeles in the Western Conference final, but Smith was still outstanding in the five game series versus the Kings. His teammates all say Smith is not only the most valuable player on the Coyotes roster — he just might be the most valuable player in the entire league. It may be too much of a stretch to say Smith deserves the Hart Trophy, but it is clear the Coyotes would have been nowhere without the great work of Smith throughout the season and playoffs.

- Drafted 161st overall by the Dallas Stars in 2001
- Traded to the Tampa Bay Lightning in 2008
- Signed as a free agent by the Phoenix Coyotes in July 2011
- Posted a career-best 38–18–10 mark in 2011–12
- Posted a 105–84–29 record in 229 career games

CAREER HIGHLIGHTS

DANGEROUS D-MEN

Zdeno
CHARA
33
STON BRUINS – D

Erik
ON
65

Alex
PIETRANGELO
IS BLUES – D

Dion
NEUF
E LEAFS – D 3

Ryan
SUTER

Dustin
BYFUGLIEN
WINNIPEG JETS – D

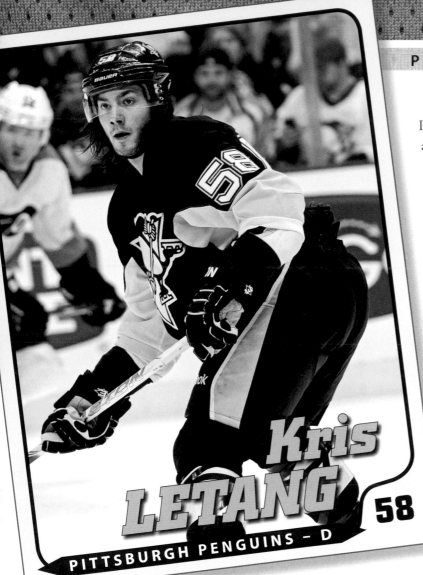

Kris
LETANG
58
PITTSBURGH PENGUINS – D

Pittsburgh blue line. Gonchar had been something of a mentor to Letang, and as a quick learner, he may be ready to be considered one of the top defensemen in the entire league.

Letang has built his game around mobility and strong puckhandling. He is a threat from the point on the opposition's blue line, as he is able to get pucks through to the net. He has also worked at getting his shot to be more accurate, and in 2010–11, Letang managed to record 236 shots on goal, which helped him to a career-high 50 points (8 goals and 42 assists) and placed him second in Penguins scoring for the season. On the defensive side of the game, Letang is able to use his good skating skills to take opposing players into bad spots or steal the puck away for a charge back up the ice. He loves to lead the attack and is fearless when he has the puck on his stick.

Further, Letang's ice time has increased to over 24 minutes per game, and the Pittsburgh team is comfortable using him in any situation.

True, he can be a little careless at times, but he is usually quick to recover and get the Penguins' high-energy attack back in order.

After his breakthrough year in 2010–11, Letang was poised to produce between 60 and 70 points in the 2011–12 campaign, but a concussion inflicted by Montreal's Max Pacioretty's heavy hit in November reduced Letang's season to just 51 contests. He still produced 42 points (10 goals and 32 assists), and his career numbers now show 171 points (including 132 assists) in 350 games played. Letang is also one of the players the Penguins can turn to in shoot-outs, and this is with good reason considering he has an awesome shot and excellent moves. He might also double his point total in the near future, which will bring him closer to the pivotal 80 points in one season.

Overall, Letang was obviously able to bounce back from his concussion issues, and he credits his strong off-ice regimen for keeping him in the great physical condition that allowed him to be able to recover more

D efenseman Kris Letang has been honing his game at the NHL level for the past five seasons and his future looks to be extremely bright. The Pittsburgh Penguins drafted the slightly undersized 6-foot, 201-pound blue-liner at the 2005 entry draft when they took the Montreal native 62nd overall. Letang's first full season with Pittsburgh came in 2007–08 when he played in 63 games and recorded 17 points (6 goals and 11 assists). Since then, he has credited coaches Michel Therrien, Mike Yeo, Todd Reirden and Penguins head coach Dan Bylsma for helping to improve his game on a yearly basis, and when veteran defenseman Sergei Gonchar left the Penguins as a free agent in the summer of 2010, it gave Letang the opportunity to become the best offensive weapon on the

rapidly. In fact, he was cleared for contact in practice and to play in a game at all once, which is something that rarely happens to players who suffer a similar injury. Letang stays in shape in the off-season with someone who trains with mixed-martial-arts fighters, and this is perhaps part of the reason why he is also a physical player who is not afraid to mix it up (he had 101 penalty minutes in the 2010–11 season).

Letang came out of the Quebec Major Junior Hockey League (QMJHL), which is a league known for churning out offensive-type players. True to form, Letang produced 152 points in 172 games played for the QMJHL's Val-d'Or Foreurs, recording 68 points in 60 games during his best year in 2005–06. Since then, Letang has focused on becoming a good two-way player, and he was a solid contributor to the Penguins team that won the Stanley Cup in 2009. However, if the

Penguins are to go back to their championship status, Letang must continue to effectively lead his team's blue-line brigade.

▶ Drafted 62nd overall by the Pittsburgh Penguins in 2005

▶ Member of Stanley Cup–winning Penguins team in 2009

▶ Twice scored 10 goals in a season

▶ Set a career-best mark of 42 assists in 2010–11

▶ Recorded 39 goals and 171 points in 350 career games

CAREER HIGHLIGHTS

Erik
KARLSSON
65
OTTAWA SENATORS – D

W hen the 2012 Stanley Cup playoffs began, the Eastern Conference featured a matchup between the first-place New York Rangers (109 points in the regular season) and the eighth-place Ottawa Senators (92 points in the regular season). It was clear from the outset that the Rangers knew who made the Senators get up and go and that was defenseman Erik Karlsson. For example, Brian Boyle, a 6-foot-7, 244-pound, hard-nosed New York center went right to Karlsson's head with a flurry of punches as the two got into a scuffle in front of the Ottawa net. The mild-mannered Ottawa defender handled the assault fairly well, but it was quickly evident he was going to be the target for any and all of the Rangers' forwards. Karlsson ended up scoring only one goal in the playoffs and his

team was eliminated in seven games, but the 6-foot, 175-pound defenseman had been recognized as an important NHL player.

Karlsson was chosen 15th overall by the Ottawa Senators in the 2008 entry draft that saw six defensemen selected ahead of him. Some of the others drafted ahead of him included Drew Doughty, Zach Bogosian, Alex Pietrangelo, Luke Schenn and Tyler Myers, all of whom have had some measure of success (and failure) in the NHL thus far. None of them, however, could match the outstanding season Karlsson had in 2011–12. The young Ottawa blue-liner recorded 78 points (19 goals and 59 assists) to lead all defensemen in points scored. He was tied for the 10th spot in league scoring and no other defenseman even made it into the top 20. Karlsson's performance was enough to earn him the James Norris Memorial Trophy as best defenseman in the league.

The Senators began the 2011–12 season under new coach Paul MacLean, and he went to Karlsson early on to tell him he would get plenty of ice time provided it was to the benefit of the Ottawa club and not the opposition. The message the coach was delivering was simple: improve defensively or get off the ice. In 2010–11, Karlsson was a terrible minus 30 (and, by way of comparison, Boston defenseman Zdeno Chara was a league-leading plus 33 that same season), but by the end of the 2011–12 campaign, Karlsson was a plus 16. This was not exactly a league-leading number, but a 45-point turnaround was nothing to sneeze at.

Karlsson's game is built around his skating skills, which few others can match. He can turn on the jets when he has to outskate an opponent and his long stride also allows him to take the puck up the ice with authority. If, however, there is one aspect of his game that stands out the most, it is his great passing. Karlsson can catch the opposition napping with his accurate stretch passes and he often gets himself out of sticky situations with a slick pass. He also can fire the puck with a shot that he now has much more control over (earlier in his career, he would try to blast the puck as hard as possible, often putting it much too high, which resulted in a missed net or a shot his forwards were unable to tip in). Overall, Karlsson counts on his finesse to get him where he needs to go and he really does not relish getting hit. He had only 42 penalty minutes in 2011–12, but he will be much more of a target now that he has snagged some NHL hardware.

With Karlsson on the blue line, Senators fans and hockey pundits should have no reason to think the team will do poorly, but hockey is a finicky game and what will really cement Karlsson and the Senators as the real deal is repeating and improving upon their success of 2011–12.

➤ Drafted 15th overall by the Ottawa Senators in 2008

➤ Winner of the James Norris Memorial Trophy in 2012

➤ Led all NHL defenseman in points with 78 in 2011–12

➤ Led the Senators with 59 assists in 2011–12

➤ Recorded 37 goals and 149 points in 216 career games

CAREER HIGHLIGHTS

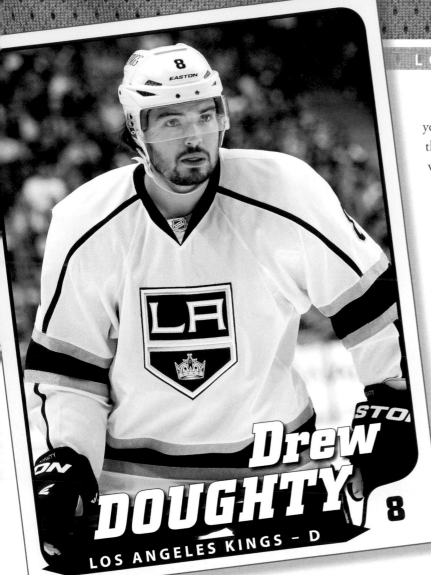

Drew
DOUGHTY 8
LOS ANGELES KINGS – D

year in 2010–11. The negotiations lasted right through the Kings' 2011 training camp, but were finally settled with an eight-year deal worth $65 million (and with many still wondering whether Doughty could in fact recapture the brilliance of his 2009–10 season).

Having missed all of training camp, Doughty struggled at first, trying to live up to his new deal. He may also have still been feeling the effects of a concussion he suffered late in the 2010–11 season. Still, he missed only five regular season games during the 2011–12 campaign, which saw him score 10 goals and add 26 assists. The Kings weren't paying Doughty such a large stipend for a mere 36 points, but the confident defenseman was slowly but surely regaining his game and was looking like his old self by the end of the season.

A coaching change from Terry Murray to Darryl Sutter 33 games into the season benefited Doughty and the rest of the team greatly, but the club finished in only eighth place in the Western Conference, gaining the last playoff spot with a 40–25–15 mark good for 95 points.

Doughty played an all-around game in the 2012 playoffs. He had 16 points in 20 playoff games, and no other player earned more than his 12 assists throughout the postseason. He helped shut down the Vancouver Canucks' vaunted forwards in the first round of the play-offs and was very physical against the New Jersey Devils in the Stanley Cup final. He played over 26 minutes per night and was the lone defender to consistently lug the puck out of his end. The Kings had a good mixture of veterans (Willie Mitchell, Matt Greene and Rob Scuderi) and youngsters (Alec Martinez and Viatcheslav Voynov) along the blue line, but it was Doughty who was by far the most notable and valuable defenseman for the Kings throughout the playoffs.

Winning the Stanley Cup as a member of the Los Angeles Kings was a dream come true for the 22 year old. He had been a fan of the L.A. team since he was five years old, when his mother wrote two fan letters to star

T he 2011–12 season was a strange, but ultimately rewarding campaign for Los Angeles Kings defenseman Drew Doughty. It began with protracted negotiations with Kings' management about his worth to the team. The rearguard had finished his entry-level contract and hoped to be rewarded for his status as one of the best defensemen in the NHL. Doughty and his agents pointed out how well the blue-liner had played for Team Canada at the 2010 Winter Olympics. They also reminded management that Doughty had a 59-point season in 2009–10, just his second year in the NHL.

The Kings' management team, however, felt they were not always seeing the star defender at his best and wondered why Doughty had slipped back to a 40-point

player Wayne Gretzky and received a response from "The Great One." He had a team sweater and an official Kings phone for his room, and when he played video games, Doughty always imagined himself as a member of the Los Angeles team.

After playing three seasons with the Guelph Storm of the Ontario Hockey League (recording 157 points in 190 games), the London, Ontario, native was eligible for the 2008 entry draft. The Kings held the second selection in the draft that year and wanted to be certain they were choosing the right player. General manager Dean Lombardi visited the Doughty household and was shown Drew's bedroom. While the Los Angeles memorabilia definitely caught Lombardi's eye, so too did the framed Team Canada sweaters

Doughty had worn while representing his country at the World Junior Championships, which were hung showing the team crest rather than Doughty's name and number. Lombardi also noticed that Doughty had hung team pictures rather than individual shots of himself. Convinced that Doughty was a true team player, the Kings made him their selection.

One of the reasons Doughty has garnered so much attention at such a young age is because he wants to make a difference. He wants the puck to be on his stick and he wants to control the flow of the game. When the Kings' management team offered Doughty his new contract, they said they did so in order to win some Stanley Cups. Well, they have one now and if they earn more in the future, it's sure to be thanks to Doughty leading the way.

- ➤ Drafted 2nd overall in 2008 by the Los Angeles Kings
- ➤ Named to NHL All-Rookie Team in 2009
- ➤ Named to NHL Second All-Star Team in 2010
- ➤ Member of Stanley Cup–winning Kings team in 2012
- ➤ Recorded 43 goals and 162 points in 316 career games

CAREER HIGHLIGHTS

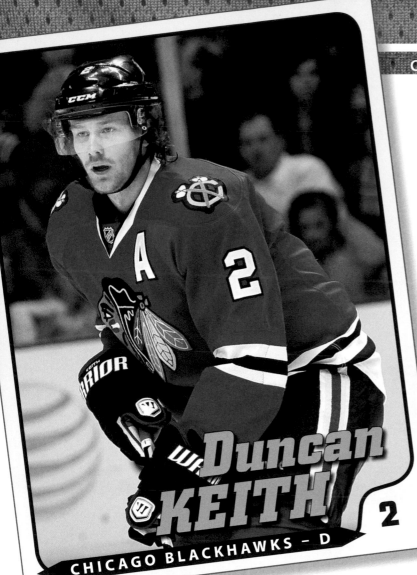

Duncan
KEITH
2

CHICAGO BLACKHAWKS – D

he's been paired with fellow blue-liner Brent Seabrook for most of his career. The two defensemen have great chemistry, are extremely competitive and play off of each other's strengths. If and when they get split up it never seems to last for long because they're such an effective pair. In fact, the Blackhawks made quite a few moves to their roster after winning the Stanley Cup in 2010, but refused to break up their best defensive pairing. With a goaltender who is still developing, Keith and Seabrook truly are the backbone of the team and are more valuable to Chicago than ever.

Niklas Hjalmarsson and Nick Leddy form another good defensive pair for the Blackhawks and the re-signing of Johnny Oduya gives the team five quality defenders. Chicago's general manager, Stan Bowman, needs just one more defenseman of note to make this unit one of the best in the league.

A native of Winnipeg, Manitoba, Keith was drafted 54th overall by the Blackhawks in 2002. They hoped he might become an NHL player, but he was slight at the time and it seemed like the larger, tougher players in the big league would overwhelm him. The budding blue-liner attended Michigan State University in 2001–02 and 2002–03, playing for the Michigan State Spartans. However, school did not interest him much and he wanted to play junior hockey as he knew the Canadian junior ranks were better suited to preparing him for the NHL.

After being drafted by Chicago, Keith played one season of major-junior hockey with the Kelowna Rockets of the Western Hockey League, where he produced 46 points in just 37 games. Keith had always impressed his coaches with his desire to improve all aspects of his game, and when he was told to become a more responsible defender he worked hard at it despite his natural offensive instincts. In 2003–04 the Blackhawks wisely sent the young defenseman to the Norfolk Admirals of the American Hockey League to gain some professional experience. In two seasons with

C hicago Blackhawks defenseman Duncan Keith plays a great deal of hockey each and every season. A look at his average-time-on-ice totals reveals that since he entered the NHL in 2005–06 Keith has never played less than 23 minutes — and often plays nearly 27 minutes — per game. During the playoffs his average-time-on-ice number has gone as high as 30:16. The 6-foot-1, 205-pound blue-liner just never seems to tire, and his off-season conditioning program continues to pay off year after year. The winner of the 2009–10 James Norris Memorial Trophy, the 28-year-old Keith is now entering his prime years and over the past few seasons has been acknowledged as one of the best defensemen in the league.

One of the reasons Keith has performed so well is that

the Admirals, Keith's offensive numbers dipped to 51 points in 154 games, but he learned to play a more defensively sound game at the pro level.

Come 2005–06 and the 22-year-old Keith was playing with Chicago. He muddled through his rookie year scoring nine times, recording just 21 points and posting minus 11 for the struggling team. As he gained more experience, Keith's point total began to rise (from 31 to 32 to 44 over the next three years) and his plus-minus improved leaps and bounds, peaking at plus 33 in 2008–09.

The 2009–10 season was Keith's finest yet. He scored 14 goals and added 55 assists for a total of 69 points, plus he posted a plus 21 and won the Norris Trophy as the league's top defenseman. That year also saw Keith selected to play for Team Canada at the 2010 Winter Olympics, where he set up six goals in seven games to help Canada claim the gold medal. Later that season, the Blackhawks won the Stanley Cup with Keith leading the blue-line attack with 17 points in 22 playoff games.

After such a difficult and emotional season, Keith's

CAREER HIGHLIGHTS

- ▶ Drafted 54th overall by the Chicago Blackhawks in 2002
- ▶ Named winner of the James Norris Memorial Trophy in 2010
- ▶ Member of Stanley Cup–winning Blackhawks team in 2010
- ▶ NHL First Team All-Star in 2010
- ▶ Recorded 56 goals and 282 points in 560 career games

play dipped in 2010–11 and he posted a minus-1 on the season, just the second minus rating of his NHL career. The 2011–12 season saw Keith rebound slightly, but his point totals have yet to return to the level of his 2009–10 career best. Still, as the Blackhawks continue to tinker with their roster in an attempt to regain their championship caliber, Keith is sure to be the defensive pillar they'll build upon and use for support.

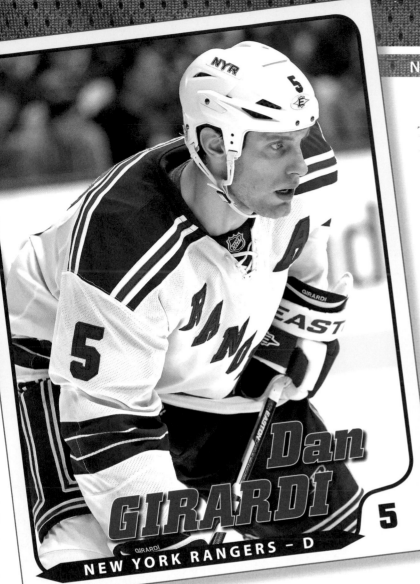

Dan
GIRARDI
GIRARDI
NEW YORK RANGERS - D
5

The low scoring but defensively sound Girardi was with the Knights when they won the Memorial Cup in 2004–05 after being traded mid-season. He had 14 points in 31 regular season games for the Knights and the team romped to the junior championship. Girardi was 20 years old by this time and no NHL team had bothered to select him despite being available for three entry drafts. The only team to make him an offer was the New York Rangers, and they only put a minor league deal on the table. Girardi's determination to make it to the big league saw him sign the deal but he did not even get to start in the American Hockey League (AHL). Instead Girardi had to begin his long journey in the East Coast Hockey League (ECHL) — the lowest rung in pro hockey.

He was with the Charlotte Checkers of the ECHL for just seven games, however, before going up to the Hartford Wolf Pack of the AHL to close out the 2005–06 season. He was back in Hartford to begin the next season, but then the Rangers needed him in New York to replace injured players. He played 34 NHL games in 2006–07, recording 6 assists and registering a plus-minus of plus 7. Girardi has not looked back since he was summoned to the Rangers and over the last six seasons has perfected his shutdown role. Despite the toll of the NHL game, the physical but not overly aggressive defenseman has only missed two NHL games since his promotion.

Girardi's career has really blossomed under the coaching of John Tortorella, who took over as the Rangers bench boss in February of 2009. A no-nonsense kind of mentor, Tortorella has come to rely on Girardi as much as any defenseman on the team. Tortorella plays the blueliner in all situations and the faith the coach has shown in Girardi has only served to increase his confidence. The Rangers make it a point to play strong defensive hockey, with the emphasis on a high rate of blocked opposition shots — Girardi is one of the best at that very difficult task. Despite his understated style it

When defenseman Dan Girardi was playing hockey for the Welland Cougars as a teen-ager, his coach, Mark Forster, could see what a hardworking, determined player he was. While Forster was not sure that the 6-foot-1, 205-pound blueliner would make the NHL, he was positive Girardi was going to give it all he had because he was so intent on improving. Years passed in which NHL scouts over-looked his tremendous work ethic and strong desire. Girardi was on the quiet side and that may have con-tributed to the lack of NHL interest, but he never com-plained and kept getting better each season.

Girardi played junior hockey in the Ontario Hockey League for the Barrie Colts, the Guelph Storm and finally the London Knights between 2001 and 2005.

took Girardi some time to become a plus player. He was a minus 14 in 2008–09 but by the end of the 2011–12 season, Girardi was a plus 13 even though he played over 26 minutes per game.

The Rangers had one of their best seasons in 2011–12, and finished on top of the Eastern Conference despite missing defenseman Marc Staal for the early part of the season. Girardi filled in very capably and scored five goals and totaled 24 points — the second best point mark of his career. In the 2012 playoffs Girardi was one of the best players on the Rangers, as they won two seven-game series; he recorded 12 points in 20 games. Although he is not offensively inclined Girardi did score three goals in the post-season and they were all game winners. He was a plus six in the playoffs and played just under 27 minutes on a nightly basis.

The Rangers made a wise choice in signing Girardi to a two-year $13.3 million contract extension, and the 27 year old is ready to give the Broadway Blueshirts the best years of his career. His success should give all pro scouts a reason to take a second look at undervalued prospects, because there are more like Girardi who have big hearts and can succeed in the NHL given time and a chance to show what they're made of.

CAREER HIGHLIGHTS

➤ Signed as an undrafted free agent by the New York Rangers in 2006

➤ Scored 10 goals in 2007–08

➤ Played a full 82-game schedule four times

➤ Recorded 22 or more points in five consecutive seasons

➤ Recorded 29 goals and 140 points in 422 career games

Dion
PHANEUF 3
TORONTO MAPLE LEAFS – D

Leafs, and he realizes that in being the team's captain, Phaneuf is carrying a heavy load. The weight Carlyle specifically refers to is in relation to the pressure Phaneuf had to recently withstand as he took the heat for the Maple Leafs' ultimate failure to make the playoffs in the 2011–12 season.

The Leafs and the rugged 6-foot-3, 214-pound blue-liner actually got off to a good start in the 2011–12 campaign, and then-coach Ron Wilson even went so far as to say Phaneuf was the best defenseman in the league. Indeed, the Leafs built up a record of 28–19–6 before a colossal collapse sent them to the bottom of the Eastern Conference where they finished 13th overall. Despite this downfall, Phaneuf's season totals were still respectable as he turned in 44 points in 82 games. Under Wilson's guidance, though, it looked as if Phaneuf was getting tired, as he was often victimized by opposing forwards who were beating him to the outside. He was also clearly missing playing with his on-ice partner Keith Aulie — another big hitter who made the pair a fearsome duo — who was traded to the Tampa Bay Lightning.

And if it looked as if Phaneuf was appearing haggard on the ice, he was likely feeling even worse about what was going on off of it. The swarming Toronto media were all over him about his leadership, or lack thereof, and this was despite his club's public endorsements that showed support for him as captain of the Leafs.

Phaneuf, however, has not shied away from the limelight, and just as his presence is front and center in the Leafs' dressing room, he also never backs away from reporters. Phaneuf's voice is a respected one, and he can demand that consideration as a result of his on-ice play that has earned him a track record of being able to stay cool in high-pressure situations (such as when he won the gold at the World Hockey Championships as a junior and as a pro).

When Phaneuf is at his best on the ice, he is a physical player who can dish out devastating hits to

When Dion Phaneuf was 10 years old, he was given his grandfather's old hockey jersey. Phaneuf's grandfather, Ron MacArthur, was on a championship team in Summerside, Prince Edward Island, and after the young Phaneuf had the prized jersey in his possession, he resisted any attempts to have it cleaned — he wanted it to stay exactly the way it was, bloodstains and all. MacArthur's jersey hung with pride on Phaneuf's childhood bedroom wall, and the reverence he paid that jersey is emblematic of his respect for the game. And now, as a grown man, Phaneuf can instead wear his own jersey with pride, complete with the telltale "C" that explains to everyone that he is the captain of the Toronto Maple Leafs.

Randy Carlyle has both played with and coached the

unsuspecting opponents. He can also be a top passer and his shot on the power play is a strong asset. He is crafty as well, and will often purposely miss the cage to create rebounds off the backboards. Fans, after all, mustn't forget that Phaneuf was once a 20-goal scorer in his rookie year with the Calgary Flames and that Toronto expects that with his talent and style, he will again return to those numbers.

Phaneuf is not yet the type of Leafs captain that defined George Armstrong or Darryl Sittler during their years with the club, but as long as he continues to be positive and keeps working to make Toronto better, he will likely one day be counted among the elite Toronto captains. But, of course, if he really wants to cement his status as one of the Leafs' best leaders, he will need to do what many hockey fans have deemed impossible on a modern Toronto team, and that is bring home the Stanley Cup.

► Drafted 9th overall by the Calgary Flames in 2003

► Scored 20 goals as a rookie in 2005–06

► Recorded 40 or more points six times

► Named captain of the Toronto Maple Leafs in 2010

► Recorded 97 goals and 312 points in 552 career games

CAREER HIGHLIGHTS

Ryan
SUTER
20

MINNESOTA WILD - D

Suter was originally drafted in the first round, seventh overall, by the Nashville Predators in 2003, and by that time, the Madison, Wisconsin, native had already played in two under-18 tournaments and one World Junior hockey championship. He had also faced the pressure of an intense final: in 2004, the World Junior gold-medal game featured a U.S.–Canada showdown and in it, the United States prevailed for the gold, with Suter playing shutdown defense. He went on to finish 2004, his final amateur year, by playing 39 games for the University of Wisconsin and collecting 19 points and 93 penalty minutes along the way.

When the 2004–05 NHL season was canceled due to the lockout, Nashville assigned Suter to its American Hockey League affiliate in Milwaukee. His season was soon interrupted so that he could return to the World Juniors for a third straight year. Suter didn't disappoint — he led all defensemen with eight points in seven games and was named to the All-Tournament team.

The following October, Suter made his NHL debut, earning an assist in Nashville's opening goal of the 2005–06 season. Suter missed only 11 games in his rookie year and just six in the following four seasons. He also soon found himself playing alongside perennial James Norris Memorial Trophy candidate Shea Weber, and the pair became, arguably, the most punishing defensive duo in the NHL.

Suter is not an overly physical defenseman, but he has a special knack for separating his man from the puck, and once he gets control, he is excellent at starting the transition and mounting an attack. While in Nashville, Suter and Weber were a perfect pair, with Weber doling out the big hits and firing his cannon of a slapper and Suter playing a quiet and tidy position game that focused on puck movement and a sound defensive strategy.

Suter's NHL stat lines reflect his style of play, as he has never scored more than eight goals in any season and his best point-producing year was in 2011–12,

Hockey excellence runs deep in Minnesota Wild defenseman Ryan Suter's family. His father, Bob, was a member of the 1980 U.S. Olympic hockey team that won the gold medal as the famed "Miracle on Ice" squad. Suter's uncle, Gary, had a lengthy NHL career with the Calgary Flames, Chicago Blackhawks and San Jose Sharks. And, when Suter was a boy, he would take the medal won by his father to school and tell the story behind the shiny award. Since then, Suter himself has represented the United States on the international stage on more than one occasion, and he, too, has medals to pass on to his younger family members. In fact, Suter's play in the red, white and blue sweater of Team USA has given him some of his best career moments to date.

with 46. However, over his career in Nashville, he was a solid plus 43, which is a feat made all the more impressive for the fact that during Suter's time with the Predators, they were one of the NHL's lowest-scoring clubs.

After the Predators' 2012 playoff disappointment (a second-round exit at the hands of the Phoenix Coyotes), all eyes were focused on Suter as he was set to become an unrestricted free agent and, thus, the best defenseman available. With the Predators having locked down goaltender Pekka Rinne — and with Weber, who had one year left until unrestricted free agency — hockey fans everywhere thought Suter would return to Nashville for another crack at the Stanley Cup. It was not to be, as the Minnesota Wild pulled off two of the biggest off-season acquisitions, inking both Suter and Zach Parise to identical 13-year, $98 million contracts.

Nashville general manager David Poile said he was shocked and disappointed by Suter's decision to leave, but

> Drafted 7th overall by the Nashville Predators in 2003

> Set career-high in assists (39) and points (46) during 2011–12

> Played an average of 26:30 per game in 2011–12

> Recorded 38 goals and 238 points in 542 career games

CAREER HIGHLIGHTS

the slick defenseman had an opportunity to be closer to home with his wife and kids, so he jumped at it.

Expectations for Suter in Minnesota are higher than they have ever been, and despite the fact that the terms of Suter's and Parise's deals put both players at age 40 when their contracts expire, the optimism for the Wild is infectious. The hope is that the new club will finally have what it takes to be consistently competitive and bring a Cup home to the State of Hockey.

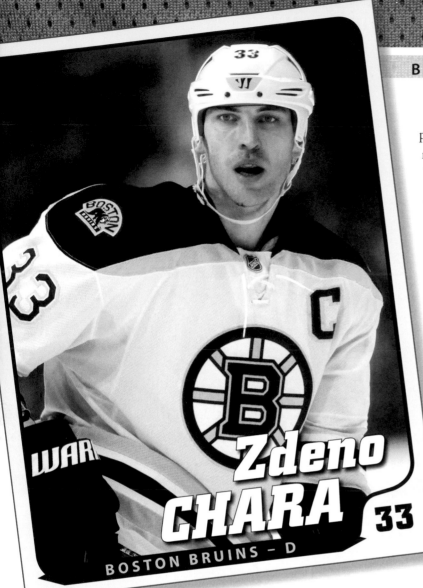

Zdeno
CHARA 33
BOSTON BRUINS – D

play for in his own country, the young Chara wasn't ready to give up on his dream of playing hockey. When he was 17, a part-time hockey scout named Jan Gajdosik took an interest in Chara and helped the big defenseman land a spot on the Dukla Trencin Junior Club of the Slovakian Hockey League. Chara played well, and in 1995–96, when he was 18, he moved on to HC Sparta Praha of the Czech Republic's junior league.

One year later, Chara moved to Canada to play for the Western Hockey League's Prince George Cougars, totaling 22 points in 49 games in the 1996–97 season. Before that season had even begun, though, Chara's size and play in Europe were getting him the attention of NHL clubs. At the 1996 NHL entry draft, the New York Islanders spent a third round draft choice (56th overall) to land the future All-Star.

There was no doubt Chara was a long-term work in progress, but after spending a season with the American Hockey League's Kentucky Thoroughblades he was NHL-bound, suiting up for 25 games with the Islanders in 1997–98. After four rather unremarkable years in Long Island, Chara was traded to the Ottawa Senators in a deal that saw the Islanders land petulant superstar Alexei Yashin.

With more ice time in Ottawa, Chara began to blossom, becoming one of the better defenseman in the league and being named to the First All-Star Team in 2003–04 and the Second All-Star Team in 2005–06. But when it came time for the Senators to choose between Chara and Wade Redden, knowing they could only afford to keep one of the two defensemen, they opted for Redden (who is now toiling in the minors) and let Chara walk.

Luckily, the Boston Bruins' new general manager, Peter Chiarelli, who had previously been assistant general manager of the Senators, was all too happy to sign the 255-pound defenseman as a free agent. It would prove to be the cornerstone of a slate of moves that would pay

When Zdeno Chara lifted the Stanley Cup over his head after Game 7 of the 2010–11 Stanley Cup final, it was said the silver trophy had never been lifted so high.

At 6-foot-9, and easily hitting the seven-foot mark on skates, Chara is the tallest player to ever sport an NHL uniform. The Boston Bruins' win was the achievement of his career and fulfilled the promise he made when he signed with the team in 2006: that he would be part of a championship team within five years.

Chara's journey to the NHL began in Trencin, Slovakia, where he was born on March 18, 1977. At the age of 15, Chara was advised by many to quit hockey and take up wrestling, as his father had done many years ago. Though he was having difficulty finding a team to

huge dividends for the Bruins' organization.

From the moment Chara joined Boston, the club became a consistent contender. Chara has repeated his All-Star status four more times and won the James Norris Memorial Trophy as top defenseman for his performance in the 2008–09 season, during which he scored 19 goals and totaled 50 points. Chara has scored in the double digits the past two seasons and has been team captain since 2006–07.

Chara plays a robust style of hockey that is very effective, despite it being on the edge of the rulebook. At a minimum of 25 minutes of play per night, Chara's vigorous efforts often begin to take a toll by the time the playoffs start. Still, in the 2011 playoffs, he got stronger as the postseason moved along, finishing with nine points in 24 games. And he was an absolute monster in the Stanley Cup final, helping to shut down Daniel and Henrik Sedin of the Vancouver Canucks. The Swedish twins need both time and space for their plays to be effective — and Chara gave them neither. Chara's most important task over the playoffs, though, was to act as the leader of the team. The Bruins rely on their leader every game, and when they were down two games to zero in the final against Vancouver, it was Chara who sparked the fire within his teammates when he spoke to the group before they went out to play Game 3 of the series.

Chara doesn't seem to be slowing down. The 2011–12 season saw the 34 year old record the most points of his career with 52 (12 goals and 40 assists), and he was plus 33 for the second year in a row. The hockey giant is now counted among the best Bruins defensemen in hockey history, joining hockey greats Eddie Shore, Raymond Bourque and the best of all-time, Bobby Orr, on the list.

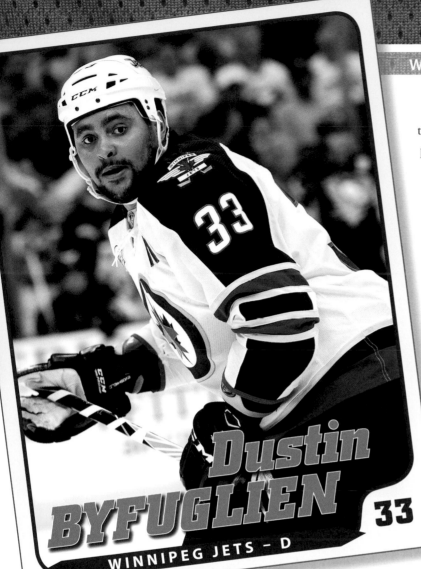

Dustin
BYFUGLIEN
WINNIPEG JETS – D

33

the sport and sent him, as a 16 year old, to Chicago to play AAA hockey for the 2001–02 season. He scored 32 goals in 52 games for the Chicago Mission, and his strong performance got him noticed by the Western Hockey League (WHL). He soon found himself in the WHL, playing for Manitoba's Brandon Wheat Kings and for British Columbia's Prince George Cougars for the next four seasons. Byfuglien was not a top prospect, but he did just enough to get noticed by the Chicago Blackhawks, who selected him 245th overall in the 2003 entry draft. The Blackhawks liked his size (6-foot-5 and 265 pounds), but were not sure the youngster had his heart in the game.

Between the ages of 20 and 22, Byfuglien played in the American Hockey League for the Norfolk Admirals, but during the 2007–08 season, he played in 67 games for Chicago and scored an impressive 19 goals. It was during this time that Blackhawks coach Denis Savard had the idea to convert the oversized defenseman into a power forward. From here, Byfuglien's career really started to take off, and by the time the 2010 playoffs rolled around, Byfuglien was a star player and a dominating force.

The Blackhawks won 52 games during the 2009–10 regular season, and Byfuglien chipped in 17 goals and 17 assists during the year. However, during the six-game playoff series against the Vancouver Canucks, Byfuglien proved himself, once and for all, to be an immovable force in front of the opposition net. Not one of the Canucks defenders could handle Byfuglien, the linebacker on skates. His three goals in the third game of the Vancouver series gave Chicago a 2–1 lead in games, and after two points from Byfuglien in Game 6, the Canucks were eliminated.

Byfuglien was even better against the San Jose Sharks. First, he scored the game-winner in the opening contest, and then added another goal in Game 2 during a second Blackhawks victory. Byfuglien scored another winner in Game 3's overtime, and he added one more goal to his

Dustin Byfuglien was born in Minneapolis but moved with his mother to Roseau, Minnesota, by the time he was five years old. His mother, Cheryl, had grown up in Roseau, and after returning to her roots, she and her son lived in a trailer in the backyard of her parents' house. Byfuglien was happy living in Roseau, where he had plenty of cousins and friends with whom he enjoyed fishing, hunting and snowmobiling. He actually had little interest in hockey until he rented a pair of used skates and purchased, on an installment plan, a hockey stick at a community hardware store.

Byfuglien showed early promise as a hockey player, but at 14 years old he was ruled ineligible to play on the high school team because of poor grades. Luckily, Byfuglien's mother encouraged him to not give up on

tally in the fourth and final game of the series.

The Blackhawks met the Philadelphia Flyers in the Stanley Cup final and the teams split the first four games. The pivotal fifth game was in Chicago on June 6, 2010, and Byfuglien played a major role in the important contest. He assisted on two goals in the opening frame and then scored a power-play goal in the second before adding an empty-net goal to close out a 7–4 Chicago romp. The next game saw Chicago take the Stanley Cup for the first time since 1961, and Byfuglien finished the playoffs with 16 points (including a team-leading 11 goals) in 22 games.

Chicago, however, had salary-cap problems and had to deal Byfuglien and Andrew Ladd to the Atlanta Thrashers before the start of the 2010–11 season. The Thrashers signed Byfuglien to a five-year deal worth $26 million and put him back on defense. He took 347 shots on goal and scored 20 goals — the most out of any NHL blue-liner — in 2010–11. Unfortunately, his 2011–12 season was cut short by injuries, but he still managed

to record 53 points (including 43 assists) in 66 games during his first year in Winnipeg (the Thrashers moved to the Canadian Prairies in the off-season). True to form, though, the opposition continued to cringe every time "Big Buff" rumbled down the ice, and in the upcoming seasons, Byfuglien's style of play will surely give the Jets a large advantage.

- ▶ Drafted 245th overall by the Chicago Blackhawks in 2003
- ▶ Member of Stanley Cup–winning team with Chicago in 2010
- ▶ While playing defense, scored 20 goals for the Atlanta Thrashers in 2010–11
- ▶ Recorded 87 goals and 215 points in 407 career games

CAREER HIGHLIGHTS

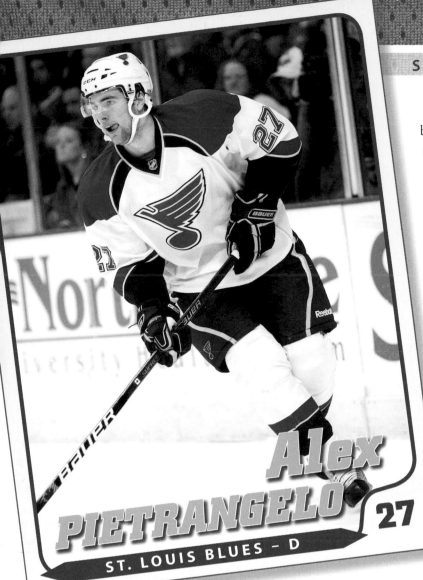

Alex
PIETRANGELO **27**
ST. LOUIS BLUES – D

benefit of maturity when he was finally moved up to the big-league team.

Making the St. Louis Blues team was not the first time Pietrangelo had to take the time to do something right. When he was put on skates for the first time as a five year old, he did not take well to them. It was more of the same thing when he began to play hockey and he didn't believe he was good enough to go anywhere. Luckily, Pietrangelo's father buoyed his confidence and convinced him to stick with it.

Pietrangelo started his career as a forward, but with his defensive mindset, he was soon back on the blue line. It wasn't until the 2005–06 season, when he joined the Toronto Junior Canadiens of the Greater Toronto Hockey League, that he found the offensive side of his game and in one season recorded 44 points in 44 games.

His offensive outburst was noticed and Pietrangelo was taken third overall by the Mississauga IceDogs in the Ontario Hockey League (OHL) draft. His strong play continued in the OHL and he was twice selected (in 2009 and 2010) to play for Team Canada at the World Junior Championships. By the time his OHL career was over, Pietrangelo had racked up 163 points (37 goals and 126 assists) in 180 games played. During that time he also saw some action with the Blues (17 games), as well as gained a bit of playoff experience with the Peoria Rivermen, the Blues' American Hockey League farm club.

Then, at long last, at 21 years old, Pietrangelo fulfilled his dream in the 2010–11 season — he was finally a full-time NHLer. As a rookie, he acquainted himself well with 11 goals and 32 assists. His play was good enough to be selected to be on Team Canada for the 2011 World Championships, where he was named the best defenseman at the tournament, scoring five points in seven games.

The Blues, however, didn't make the playoffs in 2010–11, and when the team was underperforming at the beginning of the 2011–12 season, coach Ken

T he St. Louis Blues did a smart thing after they drafted defenseman Alex Pietrangelo fourth overall at the 2008 NHL entry draft — they sent him back to junior hockey. The 6-foot-4, 206-pound blue-liner from King City, Ontario, was part of a defenseman-loaded draft that also featured Drew Doughty, Zach Bogosian, Luke Schenn, Tyler Myers, Erik Karlsson, Michael Del Zotto and John Carlson. Some, like Doughty, Bogosian and Schenn, stayed with their NHL teams, but the Blues believed the man they call "Petro" could eventually become the best defenseman of the group as long as he wasn't rushed into an NHL uniform. This decision was a little disappointing for Pietrangelo, who had to play two more seasons of junior hockey after the NHL draft, but he had gained the

Hitchcock was brought in to right the ship. The Blues went on to win the top spot in the Western Conference after Hitchcock, who was primarily known as a defensive coach, stressed a defense-first team approach. He had moved Pietrangelo to the top pairing on the Blues' defense and expected him to be both defensively responsible and a contributor on the score sheet. The young defenseman answered the challenge with a plus-16 rating while notching 12 goals and 39 assists. True, the eventual Stanley Cup champions, the Los Angeles Kings, ousted the Blues in the second round of the playoffs, but the Blues are moving in the right direction and they are

counting on Pietrangelo to be a big part of their success. Perhaps the biggest asset he brings to the team is his low panic point when he has the puck; in these moments the game seems to slow down, as he is able to make accurate outlet passes or carry the puck out of his end — two difficult and highly coveted skills in the NHL. There is no doubt St. Louis made the right choice in slowly developing Pietrangelo, and it's no secret that other NHL teams could do well to take note and also slow down the career trajectories of young, skilled defensemen who are drafted high but aren't yet ready for the big arena.

> Drafted 4th overall by the St. Louis Blues in 2008

> Named to the NHL's Second All-Star Team in 2012

> Posted a career-high 51 points (12 goals and 39 assists) in 2011–12

> Recorded 24 goals and 97 points in 177 career games

CAREER HIGHLIGHTS

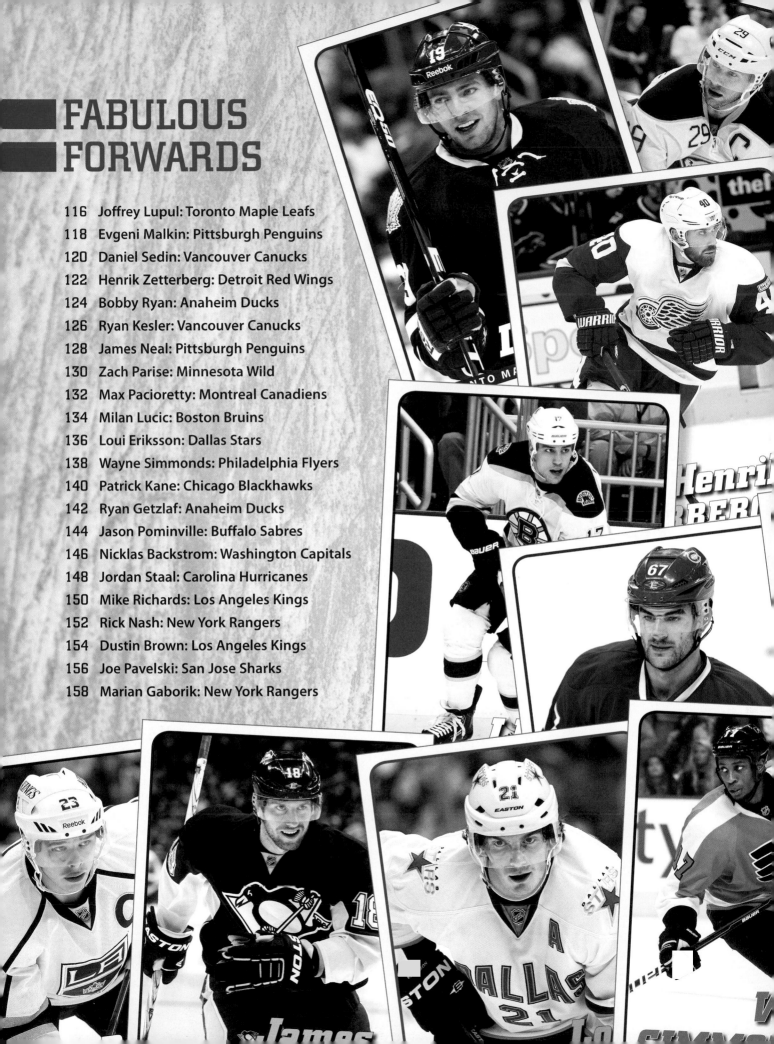

FABULOUS FORWARDS

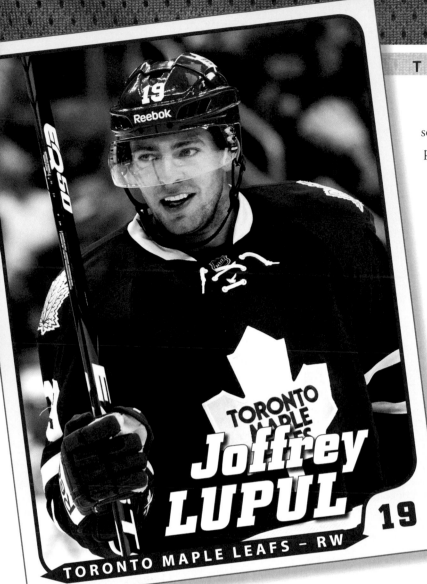

Joffrey
LUPUL
19
TORONTO MAPLE LEAFS – RW

Joffrey Lupul enjoyed a good start to his NHL career and it looked like the sky was the limit for the talented 6-foot-1, 206-pound winger. A native of Edmonton, Alberta, Lupul started out his career playing minor hockey, but he was never the best player and by the time he was 14 years old, he was only 5-foot-4 and not at the top of the draft picks for any team in the Western Hockey League (WHL). Instead, he played for the Fort Saskatchewan Traders of the Alberta Junior Hockey League for two years, scoring 83 goals in total. His perseverance paid off and he finally made the WHL with the Medicine Hat Tigers, where he developed into a top junior prospect who was eventually taken seventh overall by the Anaheim Ducks in 2002. Lupul scored 13 goals in his rookie year, added 28 in his

sophomore season and was also impressive in the 2006 playoffs where he registered 9 goals and 11 points in 16 games. Anaheim, however, seized an opportunity to add star defenseman Chris Pronger to its team and that meant, in exchange, Lupul was on his way to the Edmonton Oilers. Only a year later, he became a Philadelphia Flyer, where he scored 45 times in two seasons (2007–08 and 2008–09). But, for the second time in three years, he was traded in exchange for Pronger, and this time it was back to Anaheim.

The season Lupul returned to Anaheim is one he likely wants to forget. He had 10 goals in his first 23 games, but a back injury sidelined him for the rest of 2009–10. He twice required surgery to correct a problem with his spine, and that led to two serious infections. He lost 40 pounds and there were concerns he might not walk again. It was a long, painful recovery, and getting back to playing hockey seemed to be the least of his problems. For a young man in his early 20s, it was a difficult time. Eventually, however, his infections cleared up, and after one year away from the game, Lupul rejoined the Ducks for the 2010–11 campaign.

Even though Anaheim was familiar with Lupul, the team was impatient with him after his recovery. Coach Randy Carlyle told Lupul he would never play in the NHL as a left-winger (he is a right-hand shot), but the Toronto Maple Leafs were interested enough in Lupul to give him a shot and they acquired him, along with Jake Gardiner, for defenseman Francois Beauchemin. The fresh start did Lupul a world of good and his strong play allowed him to finish 2010–11 with 18 points (9 goals and 9 assists) in 28 games for the Leafs.

The start of the 2011–12 season saw a continuation of Lupul's fine play as he teamed up with Phil Kessel to form a dynamic duo that stayed atop the scoring race for almost the entire season. Lupul played the best hockey of his career, scoring 25 goals and 67 points in 66 games, and it was only a late season injury that stopped him

from a decent shot at an 80-point year. The slumping Leafs also missed his presence in the lineup, as the team was in a good position to make the playoffs but faltered badly in February and March to once again be on the outside looking in.

In another twist of fate, Carlyle, fired from the Ducks, was hired to coach the Leafs, and Lupul — injured or not — had to adjust to playing for a man who was once openly critical of him. Extending an olive branch, however, the new Leafs bench boss admitted he was mistaken and was happy to see Lupul succeeding once again.

Lupul was the Leafs' best forward in 2011–12 and he improved his all-round game significantly, finishing as a plus player for only the fourth time in his career. He was competitive during every game for a team that badly needed his leadership, and as a reward for his excellent play, he was recognized with a trip to the mid-season NHL All-Star Game as well as being named a finalist for

the Bill Masterton Memorial Trophy (which is given to the NHL player who best exemplifies the qualities of perseverance, sportsmanship and dedication to the game). Really, as far as Lupul is concerned, his comeback has just begun.

➤ Drafted 7th overall by the Anaheim Ducks in 2002

➤ Scored a career-best 28 goals for Anaheim in 2005–06

➤ Recorded a career-high 67 points in 66 games played in 2011–12

➤ Recorded 151 goals and 323 points in 515 career games

CAREER HIGHLIGHTS

Evgeni MALKIN 71

PITTSBURGH PENGUINS – C

take home his second Art Ross Trophy. He played most of the year with wingers James Neal (40 goals) and Chris Kunitz (26 goals), and the line produced a total of 116 markers, which helped the Penguins to an NHL-best 282 goals scored over the season's 82-game schedule. To many, this total was surprising because both Sidney Crosby (who played only 22 games in 2011–12) and Jordan Staal (who played 62 games) missed a lot of hockey, but Malkin is all about taking on challenges and putting the fate of his entire team on his shoulders.

Adding to the season's accomplishments, the 6-foot-3, 195-pound Russian-born center recorded five points on four separate occasions as he simply took over games and willed the Penguins to victory. Take, for example, his performance against the Tampa Bay Lightning on January 15, 2012. With the score tied 3–3 in the final frame, Malkin went to work and scored a natural hat trick to seal the deal 6–3. His first goal was picture-perfect and came off a backhand drive that went post-and-in after he had taken the puck off the boards and cut across the goal crease. Malkin's second goal of the night happened as he was being dragged down on a breakaway, but by using his strength and size, he still managed a shot that got past goalie Mathieu Garon. The third and final goal came with the Tampa Bay net empty, but Malkin still had to steal the puck in the neutral zone before depositing a long shot into the empty cage. In one way or another, each goal was a vintage Malkin effort that showcased his strength, accuracy and puckhandling skills.

Malkin also thrives when Crosby is not in the lineup. This is likely in part because Crosby gets the important minutes and because Malkin's game elevates when he is up against the opposition's best checkers. When Crosby is in the lineup, opposing teams need to divide their efforts and Malkin often faces the second defensive unit. Logic would dictate that would be good for stats, but in Malkin's case, it may be bad for his motivation.

On February 4, 2011, the Buffalo Sabres' 6-foot-8, 225-pound defenseman Tyler Myers fell on Pittsburgh Penguins forward Evgeni Malkin's right knee, and everyone's fears were confirmed when it was revealed that Malkin's ACL and MCL were torn. The 2010–11 season was over for Malkin, and while injuries to the main ligaments in the knee are never a welcome development, they made Malkin train harder than he ever had in order to get back into top condition for the 2011–12 campaign. His effort was worth it, as it produced great results and seemed to help mature the Penguins superstar.

Malkin played 75 games during the 2011–12 season, he finished second in the league in goals scored (50), and combined with his 59 assists, he tallied up 109 points to

If Malkin's current résumé is any indication of what he will build on in the future, things are definitely looking up. At just 25 years old, the sturdy center has already won the Calder Memorial Trophy (2007), the Conn Smythe Trophy (2009), four First-Team All-Star selections (2007, 2008, 2009 and 2012), two Art Ross trophies (2009 and 2012), the Ted Lindsay Award (2012), the Hart Trophy (2012) and, most importantly, the Stanley Cup after a superb performance in the 2009 playoffs that saw him record 36 points in 24 games.

Malkin is not so much driven by his achievements as he is by the desire to win more championships. After his knee injury, he begged the Penguins to let him play against the Tampa Bay Lightning in Game 7 of the 2011 postseason, but was rightly refused. His request was an indicator of how badly he wanted to play (and win), and it was therefore shocking to fans that they had to watch the Penguins — with Crosby and Staal in the lineup — lose to the Philadelphia Flyers in the first round of the 2012 playoffs. Granted, Malkin did manage five points in six games, but if his club wants to make it back into contention, it needs to match its defensive game with the quality of its offensive attack that's led by Malkin, who is one of the best players in the NHL.

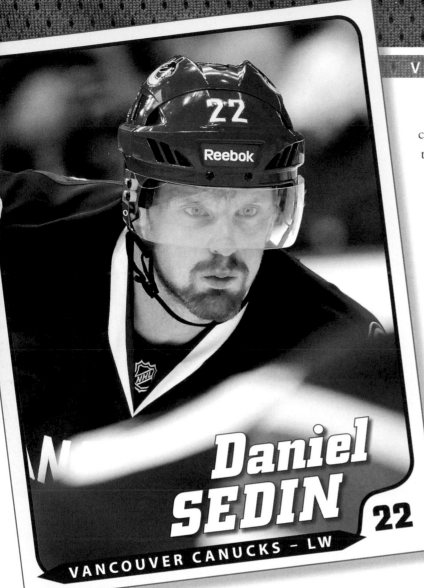

Daniel SEDIN 22

VANCOUVER CANUCKS – LW

created without his presence in the lineup. The Kings took the series in five games.

All of these on-ice dramatics occurred just one season removed from Sedin's Art Ross Trophy victory that saw the sharpshooter record 104 points to top the NHL in 2010–11.

Drafted second overall by the Canucks in 1999 (twin brother Henrik was selected third), Sedin has been a consistent and productive performer for the Vancouver club. He has scored 279 goals and 718 points in 859 career games, and he has led the team (or has been tied) in goals scored for six straight seasons. Sedin's career-best mark for goals is 41 and he has scored 30 or more goals a total of four times.

But, despite his great points totals, players and critics alike enjoy highlighting Sedin's perceived lack of grit — a knock both he and his brother have endured their entire careers.

Sedin, however, is perhaps best known for the great on-ice chemistry he has with his brother. Together, they are capable of inflicting damage quickly — especially below the faceoff dots — and they often make opposing defenders look completely out of position. The pair also plays well with Alex Burrows, who regularly lines up on the left side of the twins' line. Further, the brothers are exceptional on the power play (Sedin had 10 goals with the extra man in 2011–12), but neither has come close to the 100-point mark since their Art Ross–winning seasons (Daniel in 2010–11 and Henrik in 2009–10).

When the twins played out their contracts after the 2008–09 season, it was assumed by many hockey fans that they were going to try the free-agent market. However, in addition to hockey, the twins also share a love of horses, golf and coffee, and they have the same fashion sense (including the same facial hair), so how could they even think about playing apart? Indeed, it was clear that the Sedins did not want to be separated, and, in the end, the best way to stay together was to re-sign in Vancouver where general manager Mike Gillis

There are two lingering images of Daniel Sedin that haunt Vancouver Canucks fans. The first is from the 2011 Stanley Cup final when the 6-foot-1, 187-pound Sedin was roughed up by the 5-foot-9, 185-pound Boston Bruins forward Brad Marchand, who repeatedly punched Sedin in the face (while wearing gloves) without receiving any retaliation from the mild-mannered Sedin. The second is from late in the 2011–12 season when Chicago Blackhawks defenseman Duncan Keith elbowed Sedin in the head and knocked him out for the final nine games of the regular season. Granted, Sedin did return for Games 4 and 5 of the Canucks' first-round series against the Los Angeles Kings, but it was too little too late, as he was unable to rally his team from the 3–0 deficit they had

rewarded their loyalty with $6.1 million-per-season paychecks, which effectively locked up the brothers until 2014.

Nevertheless, questions about the toughness of the Sedins never seem to go away. Considering that the Canucks had a major breakthrough by making it to the finals in 2011, as well as the fact that the brothers led the team so deep into the playoffs, should have been enough to thwart at least some of the naysayers. It wasn't, and even Sedin's exceptional 2011 postseason (a nicely balanced 9 goals and 11 assists for 19 points in 25 games) wasn't enough. Inside the

Canucks' dressing room, however, there is no question that the brothers have the respect of their teammates.

The lead-by-example pair rarely complains about their treatment at the hands of opposing players, or at the hands of the media, for that matter. The twins understand that the rough stuff comes with the territory, and that life as the leaders of a club that is consistently a heavy favorite to win the Stanley Cup isn't worth whining about. Sedin's hope, after all, is that Vancouver fans will soon have a new image to remember that doesn't involve him getting hit in the face, and that picture is, of course, of the Canucks taking home their first Stanley Cup.

- Drafted 2nd overall by the Vancouver Canucks in 1999
- Winner of the Art Ross Trophy for the 2010–11 season
- Named winner of the Ted Lindsay Award in 2011
- Two-time NHL All-Star
- Recorded 279 goals and 718 points in 859 career games

CAREER HIGHLIGHTS

Henrik ZETTERBERG 40
DETROIT RED WINGS – LW

The 5-foot-11, 195-pound native of Njurunda, Sweden, is admired in the NHL for his great work ethic, which is well displayed with the Red Wings, a team that plays a quick, puck-control game that is suited for the slick Zetterberg, who thrives on making the opposition worry about him and his whereabouts on the ice. He is just as good with the puck as he is without it, and when paired with the like-minded Pavel Datsyuk, the Red Wings have a turnover-creating duo that is unparalleled in the league.

It's hard to believe that Zetterberg was once an unknown who was drafted 210th overall in 1999. At the time, the Red Wings had no idea Zetterberg held so much potential because at that point in the draft, teams are relying on their scouts to recommend possible long shots. Luckily for Detroit, Zetterberg turned out to be a diamond in the rough, even though team management thought he needed time in the minors if he was going to have any chance of cracking the NHL roster. However, with his strong two-way game, he was given a chance to show what he could do at a time when Detroit needed to find offense because forwards like Steve Yzerman, Sergei Fedorov and Brendan Shanahan were beginning to decline. In Zetterberg's first full season (2002–03), he suited up for 79 games and recorded 44 points, and he's been a fixture in Detroit ever since.

During the 2011–12 season, when Datsyuk was recovering from a knee injury, it was Zetterberg, along with other veterans such as Nicklas Lidstrom, Johan Franzen, Valtteri Filppula, Niklas Kronwall and Jiri Hudler, who picked up the slack for the faltering Red Wings. Zetterberg provided leadership as the season was coming to a close and it was his initiative that secured Detroit a playoff spot, which, unlike previous seasons, had been in doubt for some time.

As good as Zetterberg is during the regular season, he truly excels at playoff time. In 109 postseason appearances, Zetterberg has recorded 102 points (51 goals and 51 assists) and is one of the few European-born players

H enrik Zetterberg had a difficult start to the 2011–12 season. The usually reliable left-winger for the Detroit Red Wings had only 13 goals in his first 61 games. He did eventually rally toward the end of the season to finish with 22 goals and 47 assists for 69 points, but, most importantly, Zetterberg finished the year as a plus player (plus 14). This was a return from the minus one he posted in 2010–11, which was his only minus NHL campaign. However, despite these numbers, Zetterberg is a good goal-scorer whose two-way play and consistent point production make him valuable to the Red Wings organization. Proof of his skill is in his stats — during Zetterberg's 668-game career, he has collected 624 points — almost a point per game — and has a career plus/minus of plus 144.

to ever win the Conn Smythe Trophy as the MVP of the playoffs. Zetterberg received the coveted award when the Red Wings won the Stanley Cup in 2008, a postseason in which he recorded 27 points in 24 games.

The following year, the Red Wings reached the final again, only to lose in seven games to the Pittsburgh Penguins, which was the team Detroit had beaten for the Cup in 2008. Zetterberg was equally impressive in this playoff run, posting 24 points in 23 games.

Unfortunately, the 2011–12 season didn't pan out for Zetterberg and the Red Wings — the Nashville Predators dispatched them from the playoffs in five games. That first round exit was the team's earliest since the 2005–06 season when they lost to the Edmonton Oilers in seven games. For his part, Zetterberg finished the Nashville series with three points (two goals and one assist) and a minus-3 rating in five games.

Zetterberg and Datsyuk both figure to stay Red Wings for the rest of their careers, but Detroit must bring in new talent if it is to take

advantage of having this pair on the team. Zetterberg is clearly one of Detroit's main building blocks, and his past playoff performances make him an important player if the Red Wings' postseason hopes are to be realized. He is a player who must be at his best in order for Detroit to recapture the Cup.

▶ Drafted 210th overall by the Detroit Red Wings in 1999

▶ Member of Stanley Cup–winning Red Wings team in 2008

▶ Winner of Conn Smythe Trophy in 2008

▶ Recorded 102 points (51 goals and 51 assists) in 109 career playoff games

▶ Recorded 252 goals and 624 points in 668 career games

CAREER HIGHLIGHTS

Bobby RYAN 9

ANAHEIM DUCKS – RW

It was the unforgettable goal of the 2011 playoffs, and Anaheim winger Bobby Ryan scored it. The tally came during Game 5 of the first round series between the Ducks and the Nashville Predators, with the score tied 1–1. Ryan blocked a shot at his own blueline and took the puck straight up the ice with Predators defenseman David Legwand in good position to check him. Ryan then deked past Legwand in spectacular fashion by twice sliding the puck through the defenseman, turning him inside out. Immediately bearing in on goaltender Pekka Rinne, Ryan coolly deked forehand to backhand and calmly flipped a backhand shot over the stretching Rinne and into the net. The Ducks home crowd went wild while Ryan's teammates mobbed the young sniper in appreciation. The only down note for

the Ducks was that the Predators scored late in the game and then again in overtime to edge the Ducks 4–3. But no one would ever forget seeing Ryan's gorgeous goal.

Ryan has scored many picturesque goals over his still very young career and it looks like he will score many more. Four consecutive seasons of 30 or more goals makes Ryan one of the most feared shooters in the entire NHL, and a 40 to 50 goal campaign is not out of the question for the sharp-shooting Duck. Ryan is something of a hulking winger at 6-foot-2 and 209 pounds, and he plays a game that is equal parts physical and finesse.

It is something of a miracle that Ryan is playing hockey at all, let alone in the NHL, given what his father, Robert Stevenson, put him through when he was ten years old in 1997. Robert, a former boxer, jumped bail and moved his entire family from New Jersey to Canada and then to California in order to escape an aggravated assault charge in New Jersey after a domestic dispute with his wife.

The fugitive changed the family name from Stevenson to Ryan (taken from the movie *Saving Private Ryan*) in the hopes of escaping the notice of authorities. Somehow still focused on his son's hockey career, the family found a good hockey program near Los Angeles, and Bobby continued to play through the turmoil. The authorities eventually caught up with Robert and he was sentenced to five years in Camden prison. Both Bobby and his mother have forgiven Robert and have found solace in sharing their story.

Ryan was taken by the Anaheim Ducks second overall at the 2005 NHL entry draft. That draft was unique since all the teams went into the weighted lottery to determine selection because the NHL was coming off the lockout that had wiped out the entire 2004–05 season. The Ducks, having finished 22nd in the league, were lucky to have landed so high in the lottery and were fortunate to grab a future star like Ryan. Anaheim sent their draft choice back to finish his junior career and Ryan played two great seasons for the Owen Sound Attack of the Ontario Hockey League, recording 74 goals and 197 points in 122 games.

By the time he was 20 it seemed like Ryan was a sure bet to make the Ducks in 2007–08, but he had to play in the minors (49 points in 48 games) because of salary cap issues in Anaheim. His play in Portland and Iowa of the American Hockey League left no doubt he was ready for the NHL. Ryan made the All-Rookie Team and had a respectable first few seasons, and in 2010 he was a member of the United States hockey team that won a silver medal at the Vancouver Olympics.

The 2011–12 season did not start out very well for Ryan or the Ducks. The Ducks missed the playoffs and Ryan was in constant fear that he might be traded as Ducks general manager Bob Murray declared all of his young stars up for grabs. The 24-year-old Ryan was sought after by many other NHL teams but the Ducks did not find any offers to their liking. New coach Bruce Boudreau, who will appreciate Ryan's offensive skill and give him the freedom to play his game, will certainly help Ryan's longevity in Anaheim. With Ryan and the rest of the potent Anaheim offense free to unleash their various weapons, the hope is Anaheim's 2011–12 lack-luster performance was just a bump in the road on the way to winning another Stanley Cup.

> Drafted 2nd overall by the Anaheim Ducks in 2005
> Named to NHL All-Rookie Team in 2009
> Member of 2010 U.S. Olympic Team
> Scored 31 or more goals in four consecutive seasons
> Recorded 136 goals and 259 points in 332 career games

CAREER HIGHLIGHTS

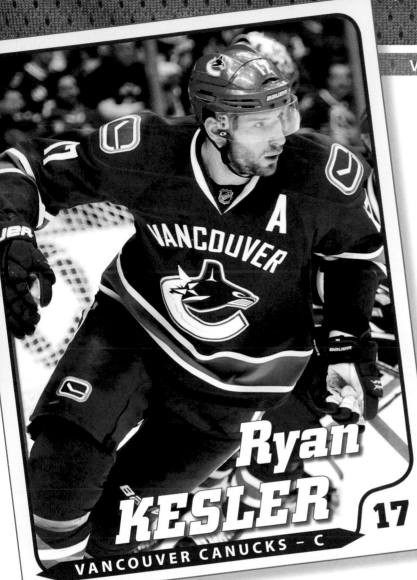

Ryan
KESLER
17
VANCOUVER CANUCKS – C

Kesler has always been driven to excel at hockey, as his father trained him to play a two-way game and demanded Kesler work on back-checking as much as forechecking. Further, if Kesler's father sensed he wasn't putting enough effort into his defensive play, he made his son put on all his equipment and pound out a 30-minute workout as a show of discipline. Kesler hated those workouts in Livonia, Michigan, but his hard work paid off because he is now known for his strong work ethic and his ability to play some of his best hockey in the third period when physical endurance is challenged and mental lapses can be costly.

Vancouver selected Kesler 23rd overall in the 2003 NHL entry draft, but he was not yet a big goal scorer, so the Canucks assigned him to the Manitoba Moose of the American Hockey League for two seasons. Kesler started out slowly, but by the end of his second year with the Moose, he had scored 30 goals and totaled 57 points in 78 games in the 2004–05 season. The following season, Kesler was promoted to the Canucks and he has not looked back.

After playing in 130 games in his first two seasons in Vancouver, Kesler scored a total of just 16 goals, but he was still learning the NHL game, and by his third season he was able to score 21 times, nudging that number upward each year thereafter with seasons of 26, 25 and 41 goals, respectively, in 2008–09, 2009–10 and 2010–11. He also had over 70 points on two occasions and was getting a reputation as a tough but temperamental opponent on the ice. Kesler's father, however, reminded him that he had better cool it on the ice, as breaking sticks and acting petulant was not the right message to be sending to his kids (Kesler was married at the age of 19 and is the father of two children). Kesler took the advice to heart and his penalty-minute total of 104 minutes in 2009–10 dipped to just 66 the following season.

Kesler has learned to curtail his reactions, but he is still reviled by the opposition because of the way he uses

Following hip surgery, it was expected that Vancouver Canucks center Ryan Kesler would miss at least one month at the start of the 2011–12 season (he had needed the corrective procedure following an injury suffered during the Stanley Cup playoffs in 2011), but the robust 6-foot-2, 202-pound Canuck ended up coming back early and playing in 77 of a possible 82 games. Granted, he got off to a terrible start (just 2 goals in his first 15 games), but he managed to finish the season with a respectable 22 goals and 49 points. Kesler might have been better off taking more time to recover from his operation, as his decision to start playing early was pushed because of his stubbornness, but it is that attitude that has made Kesler one of the most frustrating NHL players to be up against.

his skill to be effective and to be a pest. But, as often happens with this style of play, Kesler sometimes gets carried away and his habit of embellishing calls has caused him to lose the respect of some fellow NHL players and officials. In fact, teammate Alex Burrows is much the same way, and the pair can drive everyone to distraction when they team up to perform their act in order to agitate and draw penalties. It's true that their tactics worked well in 2010–11 when the Canucks made it all the way to the Stanley Cup final, but

CAREER HIGHLIGHTS

▶ Drafted 23rd overall by the Vancouver Canucks in 2003

▶ Scored over 20 goals in five consecutive seasons

▶ Scored a career-high 41 goals in 2010–11

▶ Named winner of the Frank J. Selke Trophy in 2011

▶ Recorded 153 goals and 337 points in 561 career games

in the 2012 playoffs, teams and officials were wise to their antics and the duo was much less effective.

However, there is no denying Kesler's talent, as he has been nominated for the Frank J. Selke Trophy for best defensive forward on two occasions, before he took home the award in 2011. And, overall, Kesler is a top two-way player, his sharp wrist shot is a goal-scorer and he is an excellent winner of faceoffs, so if he can avoid the injuries that go along with his grinding style of play, he should be in the game for many more good years as he hits his prime at the age of 28.

James
NEAL

PITTSBURGH PENGUINS – RW

18

on the top line for the Stars alongside veteran Brad Richards and 24-year-old rising star Loui Eriksson. The trio was one of the best in the league with Richards compiling 91 points, Eriksson posting 71 while Neal totaled 55. Neal and Eriksson roomed together but it was Richards who did a lot of mentoring to both players. Richards, who eventually left Dallas as a free agent, emphasized a calm demeanor, good habits and attention to detail — especially in the defensive zone, where Neal has improved from a minus-11 rookie campaign to a plus-6 rating in 2011–12.

Neal was performing well with the Dallas Stars, the club that had selected him 33rd overall in the 2005 entry draft. In his first three seasons the 6-foot-2, 208-pound winger had already scored 73 goals and he was on his way to a potential 30-plus goal campaign in 2010–11, with 21 goals in 59 games, when he was traded to the Pittsburgh Penguins for defenseman Alex Goligoski. The February 21, 2011 deal was a shocking move, considering wingers with Neal's scoring prowess are hard to come by. Yet Stars general manager Joe Nieuwendyk was unsure he'd be able to re-sign the talented winger for a price he could afford. In getting Goligoski he also gained a puck-moving defenseman, a need he felt outweighed the loss of Neal and his points. Neal was caught off guard and did not adjust to his new team very well at first.

Neal scored just one goal in 20 games for Pittsburgh to close out the 2010–11 season. Pittsburgh coach Dan Bylsma voiced little concern over Neal's initial slow start. In fact, Bylsma gave Neal plenty of icetime despite his lack of scoring as he was a strong presence in many games. It also didn't hurt that the Penguins were still winning most of the time, posting 18 wins to only five losses after Neal joined the club. Bylsma, who is one of the most astute coaches in the entire league, felt once the uncertainties were out of Neal's mind, he would excel using his size and speed to his advantage.

Neal spent the summer of 2011 adjusting to his new

F or a player who was expected to need time to develop his skills to play in the big league, Neal was rather quick to take a roster spot on the Dallas Stars. He played junior hockey with the Plymouth Whalers of the Ontario Hockey League, but was never a prolific goal scorer. Neal scored 27 times in 2006–07 while also posting 65 points for the Whalers, and was sent to Iowa of the American Hockey League the next season for further advancement. He had respectable numbers (18 goals, 19 assists) for the farm club in Iowa and the apprenticeship seemed to prepare Neal for the rigors of the NHL. He played in 77 games as a rookie for Dallas in 2008–09 and scored 24 times while adding 13 assists.

By his second NHL season in 2009–10, Neal played

city and adjusting to the different organization. Bylsma's prediction was right, and Neal's efforts to acclimate were rewarded with a stellar start to the 2011–12 season, as he scored eight goals in 11 games on the way to a 40-goal season and the fourth best total in the entire league. He was fortunate enough to play most of the season alongside the supremely talented Evgeni Malkin at center and hard-working Chris Kunitz on the other wing. The trio produced 251 points, which went a long way to filling the void left by the injured Sidney Crosby. The Penguins would go on to post a 51–25–6 record in the 2011–12 regular season.

The Penguins are obviously happy with Neal; he has been signed to a 6-year, $30 million contract. With Crosby back in the fold and the departure of gritty center Jordan Stall, the Penguins will need Neal to continue his scoring while keeping his plus-minus on the positive side if they want to continue being a contender.

> Drafted 33rd overall by the Dallas Stars in 2005
> Scored over 20 goals in each of his first four NHL seasons
> Scored a career-best 40 goals in 2011–12
> Named to NHL's First All-Star Team in 2012
> Recorded 113 goals and 218 points in 314 career games

CAREER HIGHLIGHTS

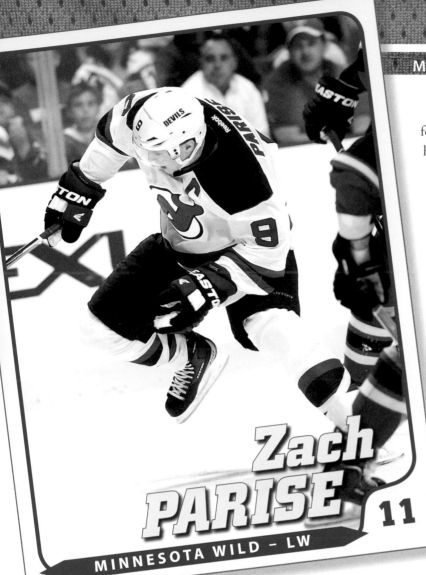

Zach
PARISE

11

MINNESOTA WILD – LW

for the man who was only the second Devil in team history to score 30 or more goals 5 times.

Indeed, the Devils likely couldn't believe their luck when Parise was still available to be selected 17th overall in the 2003 NHL entry draft. An alumnus of Minnesota's Shattuck-St. Mary's School hockey program (from which Sidney Crosby and Ryan Malone also graduated), Parise recorded a total of 340 points in 125 games in two years, and these were performances that were later worthy of the University of North Dakota. Here, he scored 47 times in 76 college games, but it was Parise's first season with North Dakota (61 points in 39 games) that put him in a position where he could be considered a first-round draft choice.

The New Jersey Devils were thrilled to have the left-winger who came with a great pedigree (Parise's father, Jean-Paul, was a longtime NHL player in the 1970s and 1980s), and in showing their investment in his long-term development, the team allowed Parise to play another season with North Dakota before sending him to the American Hockey League's Albany River Rats in order to further cultivate his skills. Parise quickly proved his worth, and in 73 games with Albany during the 2004–05 season, he picked up 58 points, scored 18 times and added 40 assists. Then, when the NHL resumed play following the lockout, Parise moved up to the Devils' bench and had a decent rookie year with 32 points in 81 games. He improved every year thereafter, going from 14 goals in his rookie year to 31, 32, 45 and 38 before his knee injury ruined his streak. His 31 goals in 2011–12, however, showed he was back in the game and that his dedication to hard work and rehabilitation had paid off.

Following the 2012 playoffs, Parise became the best player available in the unrestricted free-agent pool and it was well known that quite a few teams were going to try and pry the winger away from the Devils. Parise was even jokingly asked if he would move to Manhattan to play for his team's rival, the New York Rangers. He

Zach Parise is known, of course, for his talent on the ice, but what many people might not realize is that he is also one of the NHL's classiest players. Case in point: when the Los Angeles Kings defeated his former team, the New Jersey Devils, in the 2012 Stanley Cup final, fans could see him mouthing the word "congratulations" to the victors as the teams shook hands at the end of their series. The 2011–12 season was actually a comeback year for Parise, who had missed most of the previous season because of a serious knee injury that required surgery. Parise scored 31 times and totaled 69 points while playing in all 82 regular-season games in 2011–12 to help get his team back into the postseason. Parise was also named the Devils' captain prior to the start of the season, and this was a well-deserved honor answered "No way," and publically stated that he loved playing in New Jersey, but in the end, it was the team from Parise's home state, the Minnesota Wild, that enticed him to leave with a paycheck that was slightly larger than the one New Jersey was offering. He is also now signed to a term that will see him through until he is in his 40s. Plus, as additional incentive for Parise to play with the team, the Wild first lured and secured his good friend, Ryan Suter (who, at the time, was playing for the Nashville Predators).

Parise knows where to go to score goals, and in the upcoming season, it will be every Wild fan's hope that with him back in his home state, he will end up becoming a big part of the team that will deliver Minnesota's first Stanley Cup.

➤ Drafted 17th overall by the New Jersey Devils in 2003

➤ Named to NHL's Second All-Star Team in 2009

➤ Scored 30 or more goals in a season five times

➤ Scored 51 career power-play goals

➤ Recorded 194 goals and 410 points in 502 career games

CAREER HIGHLIGHTS

Max **PACIORETTY** 67
67
MONTREAL CANADIENS – LW

son, each rink was fitted with a foam pad that covered the stanchion (the blunt 90-degree corner of the glass). Some might argue that the hit Chara leveled on Pacioretty was late, but more damaging was the fact that the Montreal forward was slammed head-first into the corner of the glass. The crowd went silent as Pacioretty lay motionless on the ice. He was carted off on a stretcher and Chara was assessed a match penalty and a game misconduct. Play resumed and it was later revealed that the forward was incredibly lucky that he escaped with only a concussion and couple broken vertebrae. The hit ended Pacioretty's season and many thought it should have ended Chara's, too, but the Boston defender escaped a suspension from the league.

The decision to not impose supplementary discipline came as a surprise to many. While Chara's hit did not appear to be malicious, it was, at the very least, reckless. NHL senior vice president Mike Murphy thought otherwise. Murphy adjudicated the matter because then-league disciplinarian Colin Campbell — whose son Gregory played for the Bruins — excused himself from the case due to the conflict of interest. Pacioretty was not pleased with the decision and he let his feelings be known. However, because of the hit, the NHL has recently improved the safety of the areas where the glass stops and starts, inserting rounded glass instead of padded, blunt corners. Yes, a hit in that area along the boards will still certainly hurt, but it will no longer be as treacherous.

Pacioretty's season-ending injury ruined what was a breakthrough year for the Connecticut-born left-winger who had 24 points (including 14 goals) in 37 games prior to the Chara hit. Up until the 2011–12 season, Pacioretty had actually had a hard time breaking into the Montreal lineup. After being selected 22nd overall in the 2007 entry draft, the 6-foot-2, 196-pound graduate of the University of Michigan was shuffled between Montreal and Hamilton [where the Canadiens have their

I n the long history of the NHL it had only happened once before that a player had died as a result of an on-ice head injury. But on January 15, 1968, Bill Masterton of the Minnesota North Stars died from a brain haemorrhage as a result of striking his head on the ice after a bodycheck on January 13, 1968. Masterton was not wearing a helmet at the time.

Fast-forward to March 8, 2011, when the Boston Bruins paid a visit to Montreal's Bell Centre. In the closing seconds of the second period, Max Pacioretty of the Canadiens was crushed hard by massive Boston Bruins defenseman Zdeno Chara. The hit took place along the boards where the players' bench ends and the end zone begins. This point along the boards is also where the glass begins again, and until the 2011–12 sea-

American Hockey League (AHL) farm club] for three seasons. He finally made it to the big leagues for good after leading the AHL in goals scored with 17 early on in the 2010-11 campaign.

Moving forward to 2011, Pacioretty recovered from his head and spine injuries around the time the playoffs were set to begin, but he was wisely left off the active roster, which was a move that gave him a bit more time to recover.

During the 2011–12 season, the trio of Pacioretty, David Desharnais and Erik Cole became Montreal's top forward line, with Pacioretty scoring 33 goals and leading the Canadiens in scoring with 65 points. He also became the first American-born player to score 30 goals in a season for the Canadiens. The season was its own coming-out party for Pacioretty, who had scored only 20 goals in his previous 123 NHL games.

Pacioretty is at his best when he can use his size to win battles and get to loose pucks as well as create space for himself to wield his heavy shot. As he continues to mature into a true power forward, he will be a definite

CAREER HIGHLIGHTS

➤ Drafted 22nd overall by the Montreal Canadiens in 2007

➤ Scored 33 goals and recorded 65 points in 2011–12

➤ Winner of the Bill Masterton Memorial Trophy in 2012

➤ Recorded 53 goals and 114 points in 202 career games

help to the Canadiens team, which has for a long time lacked the blend of talent, size and grit that Pacioretty offers.

At the end of the 2011–12 season, Pacioretty rightfully walked away with the Bill Masterton Memorial Trophy, which is awarded for perseverance, sportsmanship and dedication to hockey. Indeed, Pacioretty's recovery is one that should inspire many to never give up when facing long odds, whether those are breaking through the pro ranks or rehabilitating from a devastating injury.

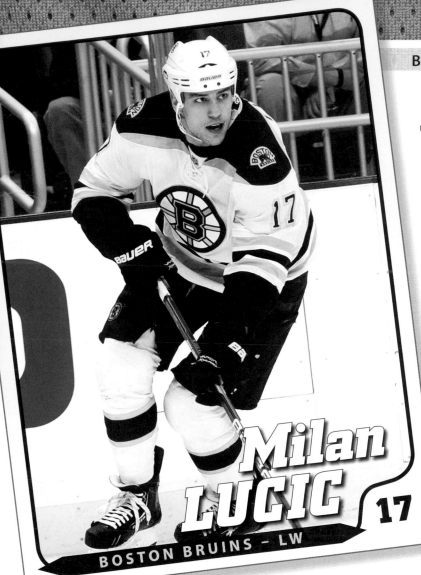

Milan
LUCIC 17
BOSTON BRUINS – LW

the opposition for years to come.

A native of Vancouver, British Columbia, Lucic was ready to quit hockey after the major-junior Western Hockey League (WHL) chose not to draft him in 2003. However, he ended up playing Junior B hockey for the 2003–04 season, and the experience helped him move up to Junior A for 2004–05, playing for the British Columbia Hockey League's Coquitlam Express. As a 16 year old he scored just nine times in 50 games, but registered 100 penalty minutes. Lucic's performance was enough for him to make the leap to major-junior, where he suited up for the Vancouver Giants of the WHL in 2005–06. He scored nine goals in 62 games for Vancouver that season, earning 149 penalty minutes, and his grit got him noticed by the Boston Bruins, who took him 50th overall in the 2006 NHL entry draft.

The Bruins returned Lucic to Vancouver for one more year to allow him to further develop — and he did. He scored 30 goals for the Giants that season, leading the team with 68 points, and was instrumental in the team's march to the 2007 Memorial Cup title, scoring two goals and five assists in five games. Lucic was named Most Valuable Player of the tournament, and his Giants exacted revenge on the Medicine Hat Tigers (who had beat the Giants for the 2006 Memorial Cup) with a 3–1 victory in the championship game.

Coming off his best junior year, Lucic went to the Bruins camp with high hopes. It was expected that he would be sent to the American Hockey League to further develop, but after a strong camp the 19 year old made the club and in 2007–08, his first NHL season, produced 27 points and 89 penalty minutes in 77 games.

Lucic's style of play is reminiscent of some of the big, bad Bruins of the 1970s and 1980s — think Terry O'Reilly and Cam Neely — as he's just as capable of running someone over as he is of being an offensive threat. Plus, he's not afraid to mix it up and will defend

Milan Lucic is becoming a very consistent and very valuable hockey player, indeed. In his last two seasons combined, the 6-foot-4, 220 pound left-winger scored a total of 56 goals for the Boston Bruins, earned 123 points and posted a total of 256 penalty minutes (second only on the team to right-winger Shawn Thornton). In the 2010–11 season he tied center David Krejci for the Boston lead in points (62) and had the most goals on the team (30). In 2011–12 he had the third most goals for the Bruins (26) and the fifth highest assist total (35). In short, Lucic is a dynamic package of size, strength and scoring ability, making him one of the most feared (and some might even say despised) forwards in the NHL. The 24-year-old power forward is sure to wreak havoc on

his teammates when necessary. Lucic is most effective, though, when he stays out of the penalty box and uses his size to forecheck and create turnovers that can turn into scoring opportunities for him and his line-mates.

Lucic tends to thrive in big-game situations. He made a solid contribution during the Bruins' championship run of 2011, with 5 goals and 12 points in 25 games. He became dependable on the defensive side of the puck that same season, posting a career high plus-28 rating during the regular season. His defensive responsibility was also noticeable in the playoffs as he played to a plus-11 rating over 25 games. Becoming more defensively

CAREER HIGHLIGHTS

- Drafted 50th overall by the Boston Bruins in 2006
- Member of Stanley Cup–winning Bruins team in 2011
- Scored a career-best 30 goals in 2010–11 season
- Posted two consecutive seasons of more than 60 points
- Recorded 90 goals and 212 points in 359 career games

responsible has allowed Lucic to be on-ice for some key moments — something the big winger truly relishes.

The NHL has evolved to the point where everyone on the ice needs to be able to contribute in a meaningful way. Being tough and unafraid to drop the gloves isn't enough anymore. The blend of skill that Lucic brings to the rink is the blueprint for what coaches and general managers are looking for when they want to add grit to their lineup without sacrificing skill. With Lucic in the lineup on a nightly basis, Boston fans are treated to the Big, Bad Bruins Version 2.0: a tough, skilled and consistent Stanley Cup threat.

Loui ERIKSSON 21

DALLAS STARS – LW

the Tampa Bay Lightning. Richards was a Stanley Cup champion and a Conn Smythe Trophy winner and Eriksson was placed on the wing alongside the gifted center. The deal with the Lightning paid dividends for the Stars, who marched all the way to the semi-finals before falling to the Detroit Red Wings, the eventual Cup winners. Eriksson collected 8 points in 18 postseason games, marking his first attempt at playoff action. The following year (2008–09), James Neal was added to the line and Eriksson scored 36 times (his highest single-season total) and collected 63 points. Suddenly, everyone was taking notice of the player Dallas had chosen 33rd overall in 2003.

The Eriksson-Richards-Neal line continued to flourish for Dallas in 2009–10. The season, however, was interrupted in February for the Winter Olympics in Vancouver, where Eriksson wore the colors of Sweden. Eriksson and his countryman Daniel Alfredsson went on to lead their team with three goals apiece, but Sweden had an overall disappointing finish, bowing out in the quarterfinals against Slovakia. Eriksson returned to NHL play and finished with 71 points (29 goals and 42 assists), which marked the first of three consecutive years he would record over 70 points in the regular season. The accolades continued into the next year, when Eriksson was named to the 2011 NHL All-Star Game that was played in Raleigh, North Carolina. During the game, Eriksson scored two goals (including the game-winner) and added two assists.

Then, in 2011, when Eriksson sat out with flu-like symptoms during a Dallas visit to the Calgary Flames, it was the end of his 263-game iron-man streak. Erikson only missed two other games that year and finished the 2010–11 season with a career-high 73 points. He also played for Sweden at the World Championships, earned a nomination for the Lady Byng Memorial Trophy and was the only player in the NHL's top 200 scorers to finish with fewer than 10 penalty minutes.

When Richards signed with the New York Rangers

I t didn't take long for Dallas Stars forward Loui Eriksson to make an impression on the NHL. The native of Gothenburg, Sweden, made his debut with the Dallas Stars on October 4, 2006, and he tallied his first NHL goal, becoming only the third player in a Dallas sweater to score in his first game. His goal tied the match 2–2 before the Stars defeated the Colorado Avalanche 3–2 in overtime. Overall, however, Eriksson's first two seasons in the NHL were inconsistent. The left-winger had an aversion to shooting the puck, generating just 198 shots on goal in 128 games over his first two big-league campaigns. He totaled just 20 goals, but he was undoubtedly learning his lessons well.

The turning point in Eriksson's career came in February 2008 when Dallas traded for Brad Richards of

the following season, many hockey fans kept their eyes on Eriksson to see if his production would drop as a result (Neal was also traded away, to the Pittsburgh Penguins). Eriksson quickly silenced his naysayers, finding chemistry on a line with Jamie Benn and Michael Ryder for the 2011–12 campaign. Additionally, Eriksson's goal on February 23, 2012, against the Chicago Blackhawks, was the 131st of his career. This mark surpassed Ulf Dahlen for the franchise's all-time leading goal total among Swedish-born players. Also, for the first time in his career, Eriksson led the Dallas Stars in scoring, finishing the regular season with 71 points. Another spot on the Swedish World Championship team also awaited him at season's end, and Eriksson scored 13 points in 8 tournament games. The Swedes, however, finished in sixth place despite Eriksson's good performance.

Since the 2006–07 season, no other Dallas Stars player has scored more goals than Eriksson, and after stepping out of Richards' shadow, Eriksson has proven to be a force to be reckoned with — a little more push from Eriksson might even see him hit the 40-plus goal plateau that will help the Dallas club get back into the playoffs. There's no doubt that Eriksson, who is signed through 2016, will be heavily counted upon to continue a strong level of play for the next number of years.

➤ Drafted 33rd overall by the Dallas Stars in 2003

➤ Scored 26 or more goals in four consecutive seasons

➤ Posted a 20.2 shooting percentage in 2008–09

➤ Recorded a career-high 73 points (27 goals and 46 assist) in 2010–11

➤ Recorded 138 goals and 328 points in 453 career games

CAREER HIGHLIGHTS

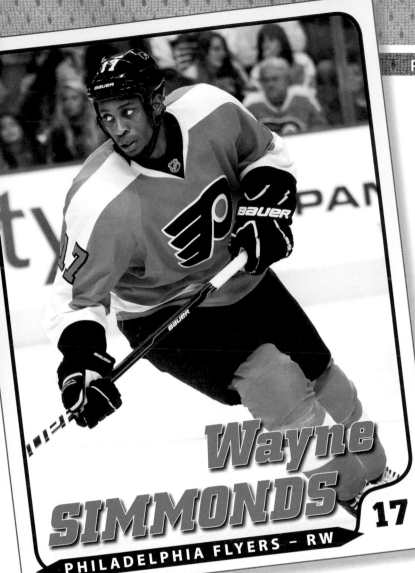

Wayne SIMMONDS 17

PHILADELPHIA FLYERS – RW

long-term project after being chosen 61st overall in the 2007 entry draft, but the rugged 6-foot-2, 183-pound winger never ended up playing a game in the minors. He debuted with the Kings as a 20 year old in 2008–09, and he immediately impressed his coaches with 23 points in 82 games. The next season, Simmonds scored 16 goals and totaled 40 points as he improved in all aspects of the game, including gaining a better understanding of his defensive responsibilities, which meant an improvement of minus 8 to plus 22. Simmonds, however, wasn't able to repeat his 2009–10 success in the 2010–11 season, which perhaps put some doubt into the minds of Kings management in terms of making him available as a trade option.

Simmonds moved to Philadelphia determined to prove his last season was not indicative of his future. The Flyers wanted him to use his size and determination to be effective on the forecheck, and they assured him he would get plenty of both power-play time and ice time. Everything worked out for Simmonds, who logged nearly 16 minutes of ice time per game and notched 11 of his 28 goals when the Flyers had the man advantage. He was also as hard-nosed as ever with 114 penalty minutes. The orange and black sweater of the Flyers seemed to suit him perfectly.

Simmonds actually almost never made it to the NHL because he was always being overlooked. He grew up in Scarborough, Ontario, in a family where money was tight and hard work was valued over everything else. Simmonds' parents still always managed to find money and time for hockey, although, it was never at the highest levels. His skills took some time to develop and when he turned 16, he got the opportunity to play for the Toronto Junior Canadiens of the GTHL. He played well (32 goals and 72 points in 67 games) for the Canadiens team, and his efforts got him a spot on the Brockville Braves for the 2005–06 season, where he scored 24 goals in just 49 games. The scouts started to notice a well-coordinated player who was extremely motivated to play well.

W hen the NHL implemented a salary-cap system in the 2005–06 season, trades were difficult to complete, but every so often, salary cap or not, a deal is finalized that shakes teams to their very cores. The Philadelphia Flyers and Los Angeles Kings got together to finalize such a transaction on June 23, 2011, when the Flyers dealt their captain, Mike Richards, to the Kings for Wayne Simmonds and Brayden Schenn. In the trade, the Kings got the type of competitive player they were looking for, while the Flyers got what they needed as they planned toward the retooling of their identity with younger talent.

Simmonds had spent his entire NHL career with the Kings and he had quickly made a name for himself on the West Coast. In the beginning, he was seen as a

Simmonds played with the Owen Sound Attack in the Ontario Hockey League in 2006–07, and he notched 23 tallies in 66 games played. The Kings liked what they saw in the physical winger, and the rest, as they say, is history.

Simmonds' mother Wanda and his construction worker father Cyril had raised a family of four boys while living paycheck to paycheck, and to see their son earn $1.5 million with the Flyers in 2011–12 was a proud moment indeed. Simmonds, however, has not forgotten his positive upbringing and he consistently spends part of his summers playing ball hockey with friends he has known his entire life.

With both Simmonds and Schenn on the team, the Flyers have built up a roster that promises to have an interesting future because also on the team are Claude Giroux, Matt Reed, Sean Couturier and Jakub Voracek, each a top-quality forward under the age of 25. So, if the Flyers can add to their blue line and solidify in net, they just might have the makings of a championship team in 2012–13.

CAREER HIGHLIGHTS

- Drafted 61st overall by the Los Angeles Kings in 2007
- Twice recorded over 100 minutes in penalties
- Traded to the Philadelphia Flyers in June 2011
- Scored a career-high 28 times in 2011–12
- Recorded 67 goals and 142 points in 322 career games

Patrick
KANE
CHICAGO BLACKHAWKS – RW
88

hitting that number in 2011–12 when he finished the year with 66. To his credit, Kane played on both the wing and at center during the 2011–12 campaign as Chicago coach Joel Quenneville tried to find better scoring combinations for his team. The talented Kane adapted well to the changes and played his usual game, which is an effective one … when he can stay focused. Overall, however, Kane is a player who has great instincts and a strong sense of how to get to the net. He uses his speed to get himself open and he can unleash an accurate wrist shot that has netted him 126 goals to date. Kane does not thrive in traffic and he knows enough to stay away from the heavy slugging areas. He is an offense-first player, and while he may never be great defensively, he wasn't drafted first overall in 2007 to check or to block shots.

A native of Buffalo, New York, Kane began his hockey career playing in the house leagues close to his home, and it wasn't long before his parents realized that their son had a great deal of talent. Like most hockey moms and dads, they dedicated a lot of time and money to the development of Kane's skills, and when he was just 14 years old, it was decided to get him better competition in the Detroit area. The U.S. national development program accepted Kane at the age of 16, when he was scoring at, roughly, a goal-per-game pace. He was still unknown, however — that is, until he played just one season for the London Knights of the Ontario Hockey League.

Kane tallied up 58 goals and 83 assists for the Knights during the 2006–07 season. He added another 31 points in the playoffs before the Blackhawks selected him in the draft. It was thought at the time that then-Chicago general manager Dale Tallon was going to select James van Riemsdyk or, perhaps, Kyle Turris, but Kane ended up being the breakout star with the most offensive potential. In his first year with Chicago, Kane scored 21 goals and totaled 72 points in 82 games, which was enough of an impressive showing to earn him the Calder Memorial

Twenty-three-year-old Patrick Kane doesn't make things easy for himself or for the Chicago Blackhawks. He is an incredibly gifted player with sublime puckhandling and skating skills, and he is also the player who delivered Chicago their first Stanley Cup in 49 years when he scored the overtime winner in Game 6 of the final against the Philadelphia Flyers. Kane, however, is also the player whose dangling mouth guard, showboat attitude and notorious reputation for partying have given him a bad reputation that the Blackhawks would like him to improve upon.

At 5-foot-10 and 178 pounds, Kane is one of the smaller players in the NHL, but he is nonetheless effective. He has recorded 70 or more points in four of his five NHL seasons, and he barely missed out on

Trophy as the NHL's best rookie. The next year, in 2008–09, the improving Blackhawks saw their young sniper up his goal total to 25. The team also made it to the Western Conference final for the first time in many years. Kane's first playoff appearance saw him record 14 points in 16 games, and in the following 2009–10 season (where he had 30 goals and 58 assists to lead the Blackhawks in team scoring with 88 points), Kane helped Team USA win a silver medal at the 2010 Winter Olympics. He was later outstanding in the NHL playoffs, scoring 10 goals and 18 assists, including his Game 6 overtime winner. Unfortunately, after such a spectacular showing, Kane has performed poorly in his last two playoff campaigns, but, in his defense, the Blackhawks have undergone a great deal of roster movement since they won the Cup.

As a whole, however, Kane has been a durable player, and if he is able to stay healthy on the ice and control himself off it, the hope is that he and team captain Jonathan Toews will soon lead Chicago to another Stanley Cup.

- ▶ Drafted 1st overall by the Chicago Blackhawks in 2007
- ▶ Named winner of the Calder Memorial Trophy in 2008
- ▶ Scored Stanley Cup–winning goal in 2010
- ▶ Scored 20 or more goals in each of first five NHL seasons
- ▶ Recorded 126 goals and 369 points in 399 career games

CAREER HIGHLIGHTS

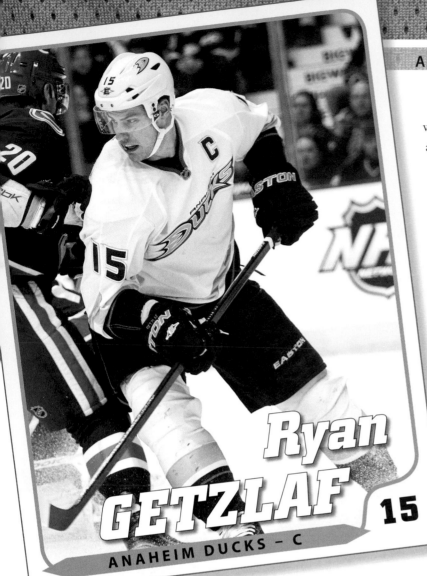

Ryan
GETZLAF
15
ANAHEIM DUCKS – C

The 2011–12 season wasn't a great one for Anaheim Ducks center Ryan Getzlaf. First, his team missed the playoffs with only 34 wins and 80 points. The performance saw the Ducks' Stanley Cup–winning coach Randy Carlyle dismissed and replaced by Bruce Boudreau, who went 27–23–8 over the rest of the season with his new team but still didn't manage to raise the Ducks' numbers high enough. Second, Getzlaf scored just 11 times during the 2011–12 season and his lack of goals was a major factor in the Ducks' poor performance early in the regular season. The silver lining to the year, however, was when the Ducks captain was asked to go to Europe to lead the Canadian team during the World Hockey Championships in Helsinki, Finland. Getzlaf

was hoping to add another gold medal to his list of achievements, which, at the time, included a Stanley Cup championship and a gold medal from the 2010 Winter Olympics.

Getzlaf was named team captain before the championships began, and, during the tournament, the 6-foot-4, 220-pound center had some great moments that included scoring the game-winner versus Switzerland after he blasted a shot past netminder Tobias Stephan for a 3–2 victory. The tournament, however, soon went the way of the season when Getzlaf was called for a five-minute major kneeing penalty late in the quarterfinal elimination game against Slovakia. The Canadian team gave up a power-play goal and lost the game 4–3 to finish out of the medal race.

Getzlaf took the blame for the loss, even though his teammates were all supportive and quick to comment on how excellent a leader he was throughout the tournament — he had, after all, recorded nine points in the tournament and set up the first Canadian goal in the game against Slovakia, but it was the ending to Team Canada's chances for the gold that remained the enduring image of Getzlaf in the 2011–12 season.

Despite his recent stumbles, fans shouldn't be too hard on Getzlaf, as he has proven himself worthy of the NHL time and time again. Drafted 19th overall by Anaheim in the 2003 NHL entry draft, Getzlaf had recorded 68 points as a junior in the season before he was drafted. Before officially making it in the big leagues, however, Getzlaf had to show he was willing to work for it, and Anaheim returned him to the Western Hockey League's Calgary Hitmen for two more seasons. His performance steadily improved until he could not be ignored any longer, and in 2005–06, he was promoted to the Ducks to finish the regular season, in which he contributed 14 goals and 39 points in 57 games. Getzlaf has been an NHL regular ever since, and in seven seasons he has recorded 472 points in 512 games.

The highlight of Getzlaf's career to date was when he

led the Ducks to their first-ever Stanley Cup in 2007, which was also when he had 17 points (the most of any Anaheim player) in 25 playoff contests. He followed up his stellar playoff performance with a 91-point effort (26 goals and 66 assists) during the 2007-08 campaign, which placed him seventh in league scoring for the year and made him one of the most feared players in the league. Further, he was selected to play for Team Canada at the 2010 Winter Olympics, and despite suffering an ankle injury a few days before the Canadian team was due to assemble in Vancouver, Getzlaf played through the pain, scoring three goals and adding four assists in seven games as Canada reclaimed the gold medal, the first for the team since 2002.

Getzlaf is at his best when he uses his imposing size to gain a good position on the ice. He has an excellent shot as well as playmaking skills, and he is equally as adept at playing a highly skilled, up-tempo game as he is at playing a bruising, physical game.

It's simply foolish to think Getzlaf won't bounce back from his disappointing 2011–12 season, and nothing less than excellence will be expected of the elite centerman, as the Ducks certainly need him to be at his best in order for the team to once again become a Cup contender.

➤ Drafted 19th overall by the Anaheim Ducks in 2003

➤ Member of the Stanley Cup–winning Ducks in 2007

➤ Recorded a 91-point (25 goals and 66 assists) season in 2008–09

➤ Named Anaheim team captain in 2010

➤ Recorded 137 goals and 472 points in 512 career games

CAREER HIGHLIGHTS

Jason POMINVILLE 29

BUFFALO SABRES – RW

6-foot, 185-pound Pominville who caught the eye of Buffalo Sabres management. He returned, however, to Shawinigan for one more season before he was assigned to the Rochester Americans of the American Hockey League. He played more than three full seasons in Rochester (recording 192 points in 235 games) before being promoted to Buffalo during the 2005–06 season.

Pominville had a respectable 30 points in 57 games to complete the 2005–06 season, but his real coming-out party occurred during the 2006 playoffs, when he had 5 goals and 10 points in 18 games. His most productive one-game outing was against Philadelphia in the first round when he posted a hat trick in the second game of that series, but his most memorable goal clinched a berth for his team in the Eastern Conference final and broke the hearts of the Ottawa Senators. Both teams were stacked with potent offenses and were the best two teams in the Northeast Division. The Senators, the top-ranked team in the Eastern Conference, were at home for the fifth contest of the series but were trailing three games to one. The teams fought to a 2–2 draw in regulation play until Sabres defenseman Jay McKee was assessed a tripping penalty in overtime. To defend against the Ottawa power play, Pominville was assigned penalty-killing duties up front with the faceoff in the Sabres' end. Derek Roy and Henrik Tallinder combined to chip the puck to Pominville, leaving the Sabres' zone off the draw. With a burst of speed, Pominville, guarded by Ottawa captain Daniel Alfredsson, carried the puck on the left-wing past the Senators' blue line. However, as Pominville darted towards the net, he was inexplicably unchallenged by both Alfredsson and Wade Redden. Goalie Ray Emery, who had committed down low, watched helplessly as Pominville easily tucked the puck past him to end the series, sending the hometown crowd at Scotiabank Place into shocked silence. Ultimately, Buffalo's playoff run ended with a Game 7 loss to the eventual Stanley Cup

Buffalo Sabres captain Jason Pominville worked hard in the summer of 2011 to get himself back into shape for the 2011–12 season (during the 2010–11 playoffs, he had suffered a serious laceration to his left leg and was ruled out after the fifth game of the Sabres' series against the Philadelphia Flyers). His commitment to rehabilitation paid off, as he didn't miss a single game in the 2011–12 season and he scored 30 goals and 43 assists for 73 points — the second-highest point total of his career.

It has been a slow climb to fame for the native of Repentigny, Quebec. First, Pominville played junior hockey in Shawinigan, Quebec, where he had his first notable season in 2000–01, scoring 46 goals and totaling 113 points. It was good timing for the

champions, the Carolina Hurricanes, but Pominville had shown he was a determined player.

With Pominville's place on Buffalo's roster solidified, he suited up for all 82 regular-season games in his sophomore year. Playing on the team's top line with center Danny Briere and left-winger Jochen Hecht, Pominville racked up 34 goals, a total that still stands as his career season-high. Further, the 2007–08 season saw Pominville post career-best numbers in both assists (53) and points (80). By achieving consistent production while taking only 20 minutes in penalties along the way, Pominville's play was also recognized with a nomination for the Lady Byng Memorial Trophy as the league's most sportsmanlike player.

Over the next two years, Pominville proved his durability by continuing to play in every game for the Sabres, and his iron-man streak reached 335 games before he missed the next 9 with a concussion received in October 2010. Fortunes, however, improved once again when, in 2011–12, Pominville was given Buffalo's permanent captaincy following the trade of his predecessor, Craig Rivet.

There's no question that Pominville has steadily improved his NHL game — it's the Sabres themselves that tend to go up and down as they try and find some consistency to their status in the Eastern Conference. Buffalo has plenty of good forwards, such as Pominville, but the team is lacking a true superstar. Larger and stronger forwards (such as Luke Adam and Marcus Foligno) appear to be on the horizon for the team, but there's no denying that some star power would help to boost the Buffalo team back into playoff contention.

> Drafted 55th overall by the Buffalo Sabres in 2001

> Twice scored 30 or more goals in a season

> Recorded 60 or more points five times

> Named captain of the Sabres in 2011

> Recorded 175 goals and 431 points in 541 career games

CAREER HIGHLIGHTS

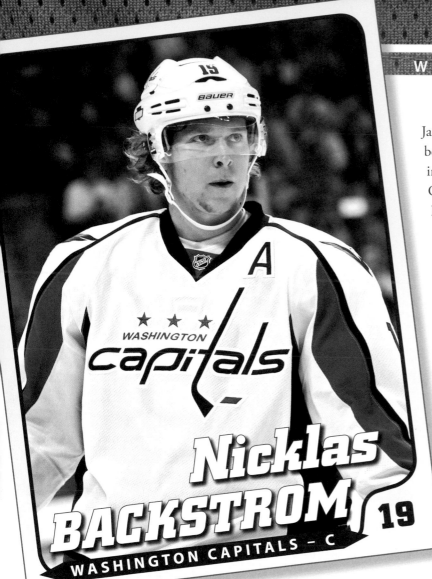

Nicklas
BACKSTROM **19**
WASHINGTON CAPITALS – C

January 4, 2012. Backstrom returned to action just before the playoffs began, and even though he wasn't in top shape, he quickly rounded into form. The Capitals defeated Boston in seven games, which gave Backstrom a measure of triumph in an otherwise dismal season for the Swedish-born center.

Backstrom's play had slipped the previous season when he produced only 65 points (18 goals and 47 assists) in 77 games during the 2010–11 campaign. The year before, in 2009–10, Backstrom had recorded 101 points (33 goals and 68 assists) and it looked like he was going to be the dominate center the Capitals hoped for at the 2006 entry draft. Backstrom's play, however, became tentative and he was virtually non-existent in the 2011 postseason in which he had just two assists in nine games. It was a baffling development for one of the more talented players in the league.

Backstrom, drafted fourth overall by the Capitals in 2006, decided to play in Sweden for the 2006–07 season and there he recorded 40 points in 45 games for Brynäs IF, a club his father, Anders, had played for many years ago. Backstrom's year in Sweden gave him the confidence he needed when it came to attend his first NHL training camp in September 2007. He made an instant impression that season and as a rookie notched 55 assists and 69 points in 82 games. He also made the NHL's All-Rookie Team and followed up his league debut with a 66 assists and 88 points in his sophomore campaign. Further, his 101 point total in the 2009–10 season was the fourth-best mark in the entire league.

It's no wonder the Washington club has faith in Backstrom, who signed to stay with the team until the 2019–20 season with a contract that will pay him $67 million over the full term. After all, the 6-foot-1, 210-pound pivot is superb with the puck and is an especially adept passer — a talent that has led him to become a point-per-game player who recorded 101 goals and 266 assists for 367 points in 365 career games through the end of the 2011–12 regular season.

During the first round of the 2012 Stanley Cup playoffs, the Washington Capitals were underdogs against the defending Stanley Cup–champion Boston Bruins. Granted, the Bruins were off to a good start when they won Game 1 1–0 in overtime, but the Capitals managed to stick right with them, sending Game 2 to overtime as well. Neither team was able to break the 1–1 tie in the first overtime period, but at the 2:56 mark of the second extra session, Washington center Nicklas Backstrom took a pass from teammate Marcus Johansson and whipped a shot past Boston goalie Tim Thomas to even the series. It was a special goal for Backstrom, who had missed three months of play during the 2011–12 season after suffering a concussion as a result of an elbow delivered by Rene Bourque of the Calgary Flames on

Indeed, Backstrom is a durable athlete who had played in 313 consecutive games before a wrist injury cost him five games in the 2010–11 season. Following that, the concussion he suffered the next year at the hands of Bourque was Backstrom's first major injury of his NHL career.

Backstrom missed half the season in 2011–12, but he still managed to record 44 points (14 goals and 30 assists) in 42 games. He followed through with 8 points in 13 playoff games, but the Capitals struggled mightily to score in the postseason. Their triumph in the first round over defending champion Boston was followed by a heartbreaking seven-game loss to the New York Rangers in the second round. As a result, fans were of the belief that it was a good thing that interim Capitals coach Dale Hunter retuned to junior hockey after the season was finished. Hunter's restrictive approach to attack-style hockey was evident in the playoffs, even though the team was already a competitive one. In the upcoming season, it's everyone's hope that the new bench boss, Adam Oates, will recognize what a great talent he has in Backstrom and, in turn, let him play his skill-based game to his fullest potential.

Drafted 4th overall by the Washington Capitals in 2006

Named to NHL's All-Rookie Team in 2008

Posted 66 assists in 2008–09 season

Recorded a 101-point season (33 goals and 68 assists) in 2009–10

Recorded 101 goals and 367 points in 365 games played

CAREER HIGHLIGHTS

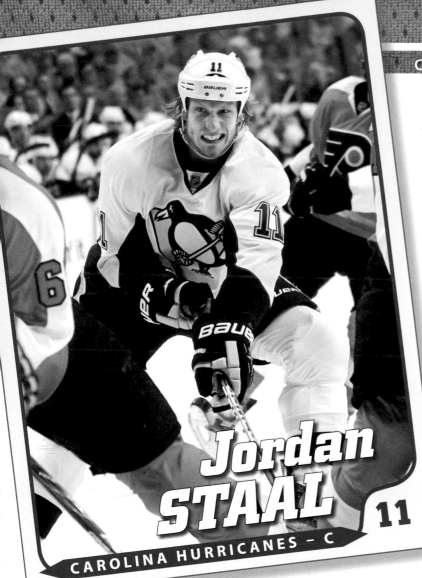

Jordan
STAAL

CAROLINA HURRICANES – C

11

watching him walk away as an unrestricted free agent and receive nothing in return. Staal was coming off the best point total of his career, scoring 25 goals and 25 assists during the 2011–12 season, and so he netted the Penguins three players in a deal struck with the Carolina Hurricanes that also united Staal with his brother Eric.

Staal came to the Pittsburgh team much like Crosby and Malkin did, except he was selected second overall (in 2006) while the other two were chosen first in their respective draft years. Staal came to the attention of the hockey world when the native of Thunder Bay, Ontario, played his final season of junior hockey with Peterborough of the Ontario Hockey League. He produced 68 points in 68 games (28 goals, 40 assists) for the Petes, and his great family pedigree (Eric was already a star with the Hurricanes while younger sibling Marc became a reliable defenseman with the New York Rangers) also helped get him selected high up in the draft. The Penguins never regretted their choice.

Pittsburgh was still a fairly weak team, but Staal earned his way on the club as an 18 year old. He scored 29 times in his first year and made a very noticeable impact with seven short-handed goals — the best mark in the league during the 2006–07 season and an NHL rookie record. The Penguins won 47 games that year, and Staal also showed he was a dependable two-way player with a plus-16 rating. His great year was recognized with a nomination for the Calder Trophy and a place on the NHL's All-Rookie Team.

Pittsburgh was a contending team by the 2007–08 season, but Staal's production dipped with 12 goals and 16 assists in 82 games. He redeemed himself somewhat in the playoffs when he scored six times in 20 post-season contests as Pittsburgh made it to the Stanley Cup final. Staal was much better in 2008–09, scoring 22 goals and 27 assists during the regular season. His efforts in the playoffs were highly significant, as he recorded nine points in 24 games. While his offensive

The Pittsburgh Penguins and center Jordan Staal reached a point at which a major decision had to be made. Prior to the 2012–13 season, Staal had one season left on his contract, after which he would become an unrestricted free agent. General manager Ray Shero had made it clear that the Penguins wanted to keep Staal and offered him a 10-year extension for $60 million. But Staal, third on the depth chart at center behind Sidney Crosby and Evgeni Malkin, wanted more responsibility and a bigger role — of which he is most deserving.

Staal greatly appreciated the Penguins offer, but it was clear he intended to explore his free agent options after the 2012–13 campaign. With that in mind, the Penguins wisely decided to trade Staal as opposed to production was not overwhelming, he may have scored the most important goal of the playoffs during the fourth game of the 2009 Cup final.

Pittsburgh was playing the Detroit Red Wings for the second year in a row and many predicted the Red Wings would romp to a second consecutive Cup after they won the first two games of the series on home ice. But when the Penguins won their first home contest to cut the Wings' lead to 2–1, they were back in the series. In Game 4 the Penguins were one goal down midway through the second period when Staal scored a short-handed marker — a goal that highlighted his power, speed and execution. The Penguins would go on to win the game 4–2, and then took the Cup with a Game 7 win on the road.

Staal is a solid centerman, and the hope is that he will be able to score more often with his increased role in

Carolina. He is able to ward off big defensemen with his large frame, and he has quick hands that allow him to steal many pucks. He is excellent at face-offs and positions himself very well on all parts of the ice.

Staal is poised to play on a line with his brother in Carolina, and that will make for a formidable combination for the next ten years, since he signed the same deal with the Hurricanes that he was offered in Pittsburgh.

Mike RICHARDS

LOS ANGELES KINGS – C

10

Richards was not created in the mold of a superstar player. The talents he brings to the rink are more intangible. He's a hard-nosed grinder with above average skills and great leadership qualities, but most importantly, he just knows how to win. Richards won a Memorial Cup with the Kitchener Rangers of the Ontario Hockey League in 2003; a Calder Cup with the Philadelphia Phantoms of the American Hockey League in 2005; and an Olympic gold medal with Team Canada in 2010. In 2012 he added an NHL championship with the Kings to that impressive list. Having achieved all this glory by the ripe old age of 26 — and with the Kings' roster loaded with strong players still in their prime — Richards is in a good position to keep on winning.

The move to the West Coast and the Western Conference was not an easy adjustment for Richards. He had an average regular season in his first go with the Kings, scoring just 18 goals and earning only 44 points in 77 games — his smallest point output since his sophomore season in the NHL. The Kings barely snuck into the 2012 playoffs, but Richards got his team going in Game 1 of the opening round with one goal and one assist against the favored Vancouver Canucks, and the Kings wound up eliminating Vancouver in five games.

In the second round Richards added two goals and three assists in a four-game sweep of the St. Louis Blues, and he picked up two more points versus the Phoenix Coyotes in the Western Conference final. Richards closed out the playoffs by registering four assists in the Stanley Cup final versus the New Jersey Devils. Richards' 15 points in 20 playoff games had him tied with right-winger Justin Williams as the Kings' fourth-highest point producer. It was a very good clutch performance for a player who is known to be at his best when everything is on the line.

Perhaps it all came together for Richards because he was surrounded by former Flyers. First, left-winger

I f Mike Richards was angry at the start of the 2011–12 season, few could blame him for feeling that way. Four years before, the popular center had signed a $69 million 12-year contract extension with the Philadelphia Flyers, his first NHL team, and he had fully expected to play out that contract.

However, due to a clash of personalities in the Philadelphia dressing room, Richards and his best friend on the team, Jeff Carter, were off to separate zip codes. Richards was dealt to the Los Angeles Kings while Carter was sent to the Columbus Blue Jackets. Carter eventually ended up in Los Angeles though, in yet another trade, so while the Flyers got a good return for both players it was the two best friends who ultimately got the biggest reward of all: the Stanley Cup.

Simon Gagné joined Los Angeles as a free agent for the 2011–12 season after a long and illustrious stay in Philadelphia. He didn't play much due to injuries, but was still a steadying influence for Richards. Second, the Kings' assistant coach, John Stevens, had been the head coach in Philadelphia when Richards led the Flyers to the Stanley Cup final in 2010. Stevens acted as head coach for four Kings' games in 2011–12 (winning two of them) and he knew how to deal with Richards' temperament and personality. Finally, a late season deal to acquire Carter reunited the former Flyer line-mates. Carter scored eight times (including the

> Drafted 24th overall by the Philadelphia Flyers in 2003

> Scored 30 or more goals twice

> Traded to Los Angeles Kings in June 2011

> Member of Stanley Cup -winning Kings team in 2012

> Recorded 151 goals and 393 points in 527 career games

CAREER HIGHLIGHTS

Stanley Cup winner) earned a total of 13 points in 20 playoff games. The smiles on the faces of the two friends as they held the Cup aloft must have left every Flyers fan wondering what could have been.

For his part, Richards professes no bitterness toward the Flyers organization for dealing him away. He might not have felt quite the same had the Kings not won the Stanley Cup, but Richards ultimately realized that the trade he once resented was actually the best thing that ever happened in his already storied career.

Rick
NASH 61

NEW YORK RANGERS – LW

always seemed to foil the Jackets' best laid plans. Had Nash known how it would all turn out, he may have re-considered his decision to stay in the state of Ohio. To be fair to Columbus management, Howson certainly did try to make improvements to give Nash some help. He went out and acquired James Wisniewski, a scoring defenseman, and then he added the highly touted center Jeff Carter from Philadelphia specifically to play on a line with Nash. Wisniewski had a poor year and Carter was extremely upset the Flyers had traded him after he had agreed to a long-term contract in Philadelphia. Carter was injured early in the season, and so missed the chance to develop on ice chemistry with Nash.

When Carter was dealt to the Los Angeles Kings, Howson netted some top-quality defensive talent, but it was little help for Nash who desperately needed someone to play with on his unit. Hindsight is 20/20, and results probably would have been better if Howson had not traded for Carter, and instead hung on to Jakub Voracek and the two high draft picks he parted with (one of which became Sean Couturier, a good young center who played for the Flyers during the 2011–12 season).

Nash is highly respected in the league because he is an offensive threat every time he is on the ice. He has scored 289 goals in his career through the 2011–12 season, and has notched 30 or more in a season seven times in his career; he has hit the 40 plateau twice. Nash is very difficult to defend against, especially when he comes off the wing and drives to the net.

Nash almost routinely scores highlight-reel goals, but they have become fewer as the years have passed. Nash has an incredibly long reach and is adept at controlling the puck as he powers toward the opposition's net. If there is any flaw in Nash's game it is inconsistency, which can perhaps be accounted for by a lack of sufficient support. Nash has been outstanding since the Blue Jackets made the native of Brampton, Ontario, the first

With the exception of the 2008–09 season, which saw the Columbus Blue Jackets make the playoffs for the first time in team history, the franchise has routinely underperformed since entering the National Hockey League during the 2000–01 campaign. Left-winger Rick Nash had the chance to escape the blundering club in July of 2008, but he believed in the program and direction of the club and decided to re-sign with the Blue Jackets, thus making a strong statement and commitment all at once. The eight-year deal was worth $62.4 million, a sum that was only fair for the services of a 6-foot-4, 216-pound powerhouse player.

Columbus general manager Scott Howson promised to build a playoff contender, yet unexpected pitfalls

choice of the 2002 entry draft. He is still the best player to come out of that draft, but outside of his success with Team Canada at the 2010 Winter Olympics where he contributed strongly to the gold medal victory, Nash has rarely had the opportunity to play in important games. He has appeared in just four playoff games, recording three points, which reflects entirely on the Blue Jackets organization rather than Nash's effectiveness.

Things are sure to improve for Nash in 2012–13. In the 2012 offseason, Howson finally pulled the trigger on a trade for the big left-winger after he had requested to be moved prior to the end of the 2011–12 season. Howson dealt Nash to the New York Rangers, who were two wins away from the Stanley Cup final in 2011–12.

New York is stacked with top-end talent from the net out, including Henrik Lundqvist in goal, Marc Staal and Dan Girardi on defense, as well as high-scoring forwards Brad Richards and Marian Gaborik. With the addition of Nash, many are picking the Rangers as Stanley Cup favorites. Only time will tell if Nash and his new unit will gel, and if Nash has what it takes to perform in the playoffs on America's biggest stage.

> Drafted 1st overall by the Columbus Blue Jackets in 2002

> Led the NHL in goals scored with 41 in 2003–04

> Scored 30 or more goals seven times

> Member of Canadian gold-medal-winning team at the 2010 Winter Olympics

> Recorded 289 goals and 547 points in 674 career games

CAREER HIGHLIGHTS

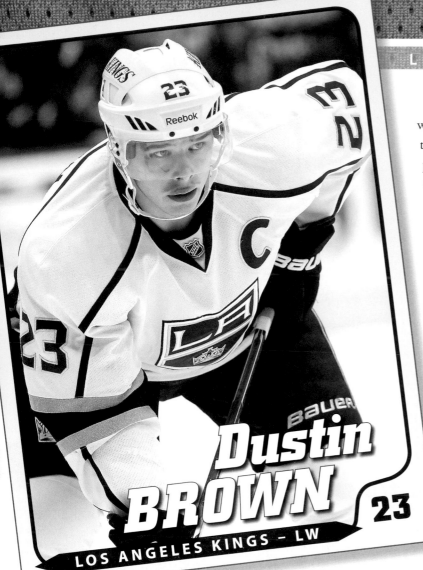

Dustin BROWN 23

LOS ANGELES KINGS – LW

was made, and it worked well enough for the squad to go 27–15–11 the rest of the way and snag the final playoff spot in the Western Conference. Despite the up and down nature of the regular season, Brown scored 22 goals and totaled 54 points — marks that were not far off his usual standards over an 82-game schedule. However Brown was tremendous during the Kings' 16–4 run to the Stanley Cup and it all began with Brown taking charge in the first round against the Vancouver Canucks.

The Canucks had finished on top of the Western Conference over the course of the regular season and were looking to get back to the final, where the year previous they had come within one win of hoisting the Stanley Cup. The series opened in Vancouver and Brown contributed an empty net marker to secure a 4–2 victory. In the second game Brown scored twice (one of them short-handed) and added one assist in another 4–2 triumph.

It was on the night of April 15th, back home in Los Angeles, that Brown made his strongest statement when he hit Vancouver captain Henrik Sedin with a thunderous bodycheck that was clean and extremely effective at setting the tone. The Kings won that game 1–0 and eventually took the series in five games. It was the first time the Kings had won a playoff series in 11 years. Brown was solid throughout the post-season and when he was not scoring he was hitting everything in sight and causing havoc for the opposition. The Phoenix Coyotes were incredibly angry at Brown when he kneed defenseman Michal Rozsival in overtime, just before the Kings scored to gain a spot in the final — playing on the edge of the rule book is a part of Brown's game.

On the night the Kings clinched the title, Brown scored the opening goal and assisted on two others including the eventual Cup winner by Jeff Carter. Even though Kings' goaltender Jonathan Quick was the runaway favorite for the Conn Smythe Trophy, Brown was certainly in the conversation for playoff MVP.

The Los Angeles Kings will never admit that they almost traded away team captain Dustin Brown at the 2011–12 trade deadline, now that they have won the Stanley Cup. The Kings, struggling to even make the playoffs at the time, likely listened closely to the many offers made for their leader, but in the end they rejected them all. It was the wisest move they made because Brown would go on to record 20 points in 20 playoff games to help lead the team to their first ever Stanley Cup — something they had been competing for since their inaugural NHL season in 1967.

The fact that Brown was on offer was likely a result of the Kings' inability to get going during the 2011–12 season, and because he would secure a good return. Los Angeles was only 13–12–4 before a coaching change

The best part of Brown's game is his willingness to do whatever it takes to win. His face is often battle scarred, but each bruise and cut seems to be a badge of honor for the native of Ithica, New York. The 6-foot, 209-pound winger is very workmanlike in his approach to the game, and although he has a very good shot, the majority of his goals come from in close. He is fearless in front of the goalmouth and for a player as physical as Brown can be, his penalty minute total has never gone beyond 80 minutes in one season.

Brown has also learned a great deal about being a team captain, a role he was thrust into when he was just 22 years old. Los Angeles management had to point out to Brown that he must lead by example and control his emotions on the ice. All through the 2012 playoffs

> Drafted 13th overall by the Los Angeles Kings in 2003

> Scored 20 or more goals five times

> Named captain of the Kings in 2008

> Recorded 20 points (8 goals and 12 assists) in 20 playoff games in 2012

> Recorded 163 goals and 359 points in 595 career games

CAREER HIGHLIGHTS

Brown not only kept his emotions under control, but he played with swagger. His cool confidence permeated the dressing room, and as the Kings continued to knock off higher seeded teams, the club's belief in themselves continued to grow. Brown's Los Angeles Kings are the first-ever 8th seeded team to win the Stanley Cup.

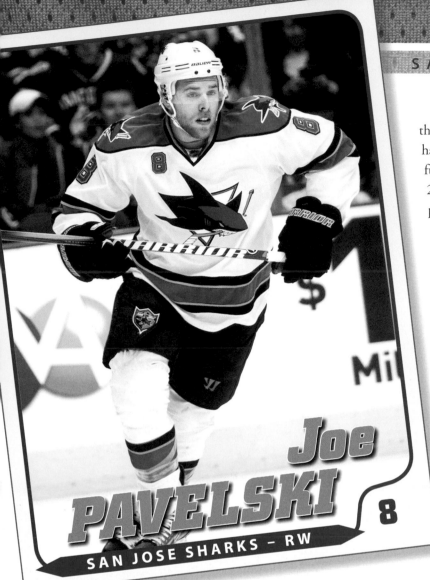

Joe PAVELSKI 8

SAN JOSE SHARKS – RW

that you can't score if you don't shoot the puck. He has never taken less than 200 shots on the net in any full season as a Shark, and he hit the net a career high 282 times in 2010–11. He is also very deadly on the power-play and, through the 2011–12 season, has recorded 43 of his 134 career goals enjoying the extra man.

Pavelski has come a long way considering he was drafted 205th overall by the San Jose Sharks in 2003. The native of Plover, Wisconsin, first came to prominence in high school when he played for Stevens Point Area high school and helped them win the 2002 Wisconsin state championship. He went on to play for the Waterloo (Iowa) Black Hawks of the United States Hockey League (USHL) for a couple of years, making the All-Rookie and All-Star teams in his first season which saw him score 36 times in 50 games during the 2002–03 campaign. His solid performance got him drafted by the Sharks, but there was little else to go on, making his late round selection understandable.

San Jose sent him back to the USHL for 2003–04, and in his second year in Waterloo he managed to score 21 goals and then helped the Black Hawks win the USHL championship with 12 points in 12 playoff contests. He later attended the University of Wisconsin for two seasons where he gained All-Star status once again, scoring 39 goals and 101 points in 84 career games. He split the 2006–07 season between San Jose's American Hockey League affiliate in Worchester, Massachusetts — where he scored 26 points in 16 games — and the Sharks, where he collected 14 goals in 46 games. He has remained on the San Jose roster ever since.

Pavelski's first full NHL season, 2007–08, saw him score 19 times and total 40 points in 82 games, and he was even better in 2008–09 when he scored 25 times and upped his point total to 59. The 2009–10 season had Pavelski score 25 once again (in only 67 games played) and he was thrilled to be selected to the 2010

The San Jose Sharks team has always placed a high premium on the performance of forwards Joe Thornton and Patrick Marleau. The two veterans have done about as much as they can during the regular season and they need some assistance if they are to survive the rigors of the playoffs following the 82-game regular schedule. Enter 27-year-old Joe Pavelski — the most reliable of San Jose's next crop of forwards — who has put together four solid consecutive seasons and is very willing to go to dangerous spots on the ice to score goals and rack up points. In 2011–12 he notched a career best 31 goals and recorded 61 points to finish with the fourth best team total.

Pavelski is a very creative player who can make a nifty play if he wants, but he more often practices the maxim

U.S. Olympic Team. Although he did not score a goal, he did register three assists in six games. The international experience gave Pavelski a boost of confidence as the Sharks began the 2010 NHL playoffs. In a six game series against the Colorado Avalanche, Pavelski led his team with five goals and three assists. He seemed to thrive on the excitement of the home crowd in San Jose and he relished the playoff pressure — something that could not be said of some of his more highly paid and higher profile teammates.

Pavelski continued his hot streak into the next series against Detroit with four more goals, as the Sharks dispatched the Red Wings in five games. However the Sharks were no match for the Chicago Blackhawks in the Western Conference final. Still, the 2010 playoffs brought out the best of Pavelski's game on an almost nightly basis and he finished with 17 points in 15 games. He had 10 points in 18 games during the 2011 playoffs, which makes his lack of production in the 2012 playoffs a bit of a mystery.

San Jose will need to see Pavelski recapture his playoff magic in the next post-season if they hope to reach the Stanley Cup final.

> Drafted 205th overall by the San Jose Sharks in 2003

> Scored 20 or more goals four times

> Recorded over 50 points in a season four times

> Scored a career-best 31 times in 2011–12

> Recorded 134 goals and 305 points in 431 career games

CAREER HIGHLIGHTS

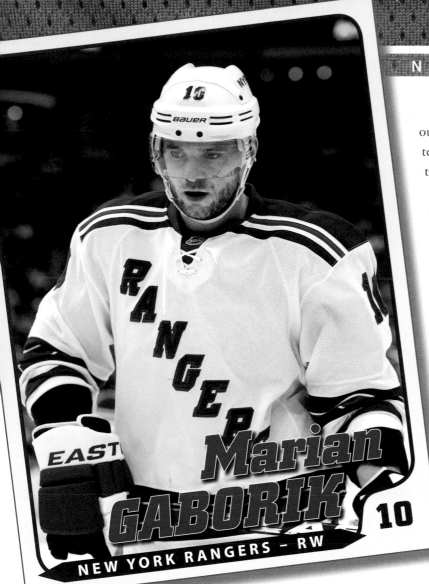

Marian
GABORIK

NEW YORK RANGERS – RW

10

outstanding performance was that he beat Rangers teammate Henrik Lundqvist for his first goal just over ten minutes into the contest.

Gaborik and Lundqvist had been playfully trash talking each other via their Twitter accounts prior to the contest. The netminder had to give credit to the Rangers winger when the game was over and the Czechoslovakian born Gaborik was named the MVP of the game with a four-point (three goals, one assist) afternoon. Lundqvist complained how-ever that Gaborik was so well set up by his All-Star teammates that all he had to do was put the puck into an open net. The fact is that over their careers Gaborik has beaten Lundqvist many times — in fact, his scoring percentage is 40%. Now, while it is a limited sample, and including the All-Star Game, Gaborik has taken a total of 20 shots at Lundqvist in game action and scored a total of eight goals.

While perhaps skewed, those stats speak volumes about Gaborik, who when healthy is one of the best pure goal scorers in the league. Since he was drafted third overall by the Minnesota Wild at the 2000 NHL entry draft, the winger has recorded 324 career goals and 323 assists in just 722 career games through the end of the 2011–12 season. He scored 18 times as a rookie in 2000–01 and has scored 30 or more goals eight times.

In 2011–12, Gaborik lead the Rangers in goals with 42 (the third highest total in the NHL) and points with 76 in 82 games played. It was his production that gave the offensively challenged Rangers some much needed spark. The Rangers were able to finish on top of the Eastern Conference with 109 points, but without question the Blueshirts would not be the best team in the conference without Gaborik's excellent numbers.

Injuries have taken their toll on Gaborik over the years and they tend to slow him down both physically and mentally. Nagging issues have made Gaborik less effective than his talents allow. He is as offensively gifted as any player in the league but he does not bring

Year after year, the NHL All-Star Game delights those who crave binge offense. All the skilled players attending the contest are free of the tight checking that has come to dominate regular contests and despite the top-flight goaltending, they can score almost at will. The 2012 All-Star Game was played in Ottawa and much of the pre-game talk centered around Ottawa Senators forward Daniel Alfredsson, who many speculated might have been playing in his last All-Star Game. By the time the game was over the talk had switched to another European star named Marian Gaborik. The New York Rangers sniper potted three early goals, leading the team captained by Zdeno Chara to a 12–9 victory over the team captained by Alfredsson. What was most interesting about Gaborik's

his most aggressive game to the rink every night. Too often the Rangers are stuck wondering which version of Gaborik will show up come game time. But, when he is hot, there is no better attacker in the game than the 6-foot-1, 204-pound right-winger.

If there is one knock on Gaborik it is that he can disappear come playoff time. In his 11-year NHL career he has only been to the playoffs five times. His best postseason was his first in 2003 with the Wild, in which he put up 17 points in 18 games. Overall he has only 35 points in 54 playoff games, and his play in the 2012 post-season was less than inspiring. He did mange 10 points in 20 games played and scored a key triple overtime goal against the Washington Capitals (the fifth longest game in Rangers history), but that was the end of his impact on the playoffs. The New York team needed him to produce against the New Jersey Devils in the Eastern Conference final, but it never happened.

The Rangers spent big money ($7.5 million per season) to bring the 29-year-old Gaborik to the

Rangers, and paid even more to get him a top-flight center in Brad Richards. The on-ice chemistry between the two stars took some time to develop, and then it seemed to disappear as the post-season moved along. With another big contract in Rick Nash now on the wing, the Rangers are hoping a little friendly competition can go a long way — will Nash and Gaborik be the next pair of Rangers to publicly debate who's best on Twitter?

- Drafted 3rd overall by the Minnesota Wild in 2000
- Scored 30 or more goals seven times
- Recorded a career-high 86 points (42 goals and 44 assists) in 2009–10
- Scored 90 career power-play goals and 58 game-winning goals
- Recorded 324 goals and 647 points in 722 career games

CAREER HIGHLIGHTS

YOUNG GUNS

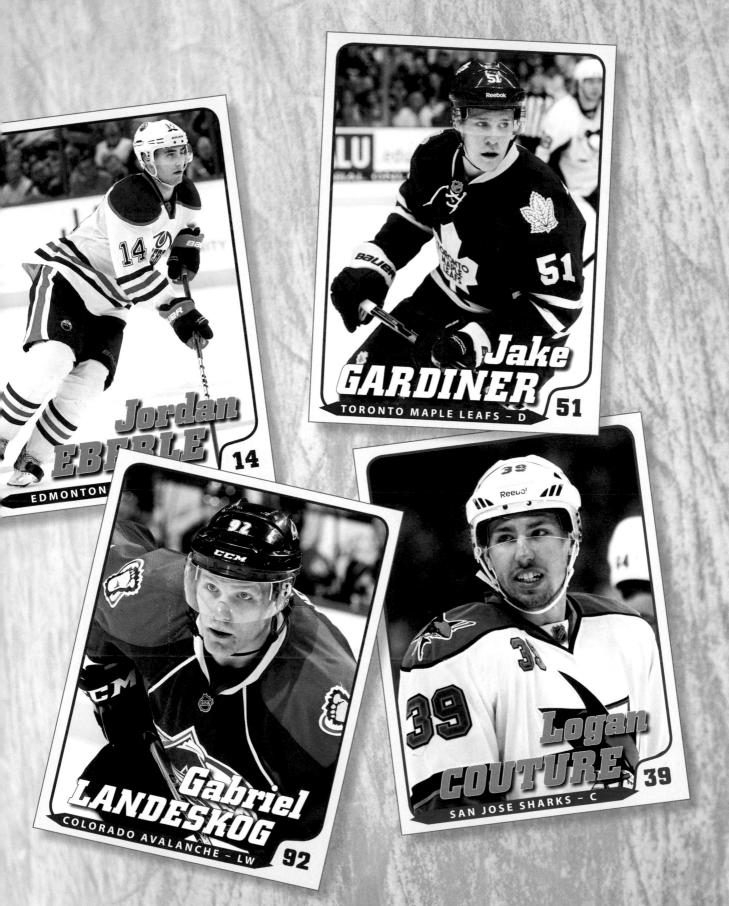

Tyler SEGUIN 19
BOSTON BRUINS – C

Center Tyler Seguin has been a very good hockey player from the moment he took up the game. The Brampton, Ontario, native played with and against some of the best players while growing up, but his breakout year came in 2007 when he was 16 years old and landed a spot with the Toronto Young Nationals of the Greater Toronto Hockey League.

Seguin earned 86 points (39 goals and 47 assists) in just 51 games during that 2007–08 season — a performance good enough to get him selected by the Plymouth Whalers of the Ontario Hockey League (OHL), where he continued to star for the next two seasons, scoring a combined 173 points in 124 games. In 2009–10 Seguin was named the best player in the OHL, and NHL scouts were becoming more and more

aware of just how good he really was. Pundits had narrowed it down between Seguin and fellow OHLer Taylor Hall as to who would be selected first overall at the 2010 NHL entry draft.

Historically, the players who are drafted first and second tend to go to teams that have performed poorly the previous season. That was certainly the case for Hall, who was selected first overall by the lowly Edmonton Oilers. Seguin's fate, though, was quite different because, despite having finished in sixth place in the Eastern Conference the previous year, the Boston Bruins held the second pick. Boston had acquired the pick in a 2009 deal with the Toronto Maple Leafs that saw Phil Kessel traded to Toronto. After the Leafs sunk to the bottom of the league (29th overall) in 2009–10, the pick the Bruins acquired was suddenly near the front of the pack — and for that, Seguin certainly benefited as he was able to join a contender right away.

The Bruins' management team approached Seguin's 2010–11 rookie campaign carefully. Rather than sending their top pick to the minors for further seasoning, they elected to keep him with the big club, carefully managing his appearances. The young center appeared in 74 games that first season, earning 22 points (11 goals and 11 assists) and averaging 12:13 of ice time per game over the regular season. Come the playoffs, though, Seguin was in the press box for the first two rounds. It wasn't until the Bruins faced the Tampa Bay Lightning in the Eastern Conference final that coach Claude Julien turned to his young star. Seguin responded with a tremendous effort, scoring a goal in his first game, a 5–2 Game 1 loss by Boston. He then notched two goals and two assists in Game 2 to help Boston win 6–5 and tie the series. Seguin played a total of 13 games in the playoffs, garnering seven points and a plus-5 rating as his team went on to win the Stanley Cup.

If there were any concerns about Seguin being a flash-in-the-pan type of player they were surely put to rest

after his performance during the 2011–12 season. The second-year pro led his team in scoring with 67 points (29 goals and 38 assists) and was one of the best players in the league. His plus-34 rating tied him for the second-best mark in the NHL, just behind teammate Patrice Bergeron, who recorded a plus 36.

Under coach Claude Julien the Bruins play a balanced game that stresses defensive awareness — and Seguin has obviously learned his defensive lessons well. His remarkable turnaround from a minus 4 in 2010–11 speaks to the maturity the young Bruin brings to the rink. Still full of youthful vim, Seguin has worked hard on picking his spots and making informed decisions. He

CAREER HIGHLIGHTS

- Drafted 2nd overall by the Boston Bruins in 2010
- Member of Stanley Cup–winning Bruins team in 2011
- Led the Bruins in scoring with 67 points in 2011–12
- Posted a plus-34 rating in 2011–12
- Recorded 40 goals and 89 points in 155 career games

uses his teammates well and has found a comfort zone where he can recognize scoring situations and, when the time is right, exploit them with his great one-on-one skill.

Seguin has never been the toughest competitor. While he can get physical, he truly shines when lined up with a rugged winger, such as Bruins right-winger Nathan Horton and left-winger Milan Lucic, who go to the dirty areas and create havoc, causing turnovers and creating plays that turn into scoring opportunities for Seguin. At only 21 years old, Seguin has both the skill and the work ethic to become a superstar, and while Toronto fans lament what could have been, Boston fans can't wait to see what he will do next.

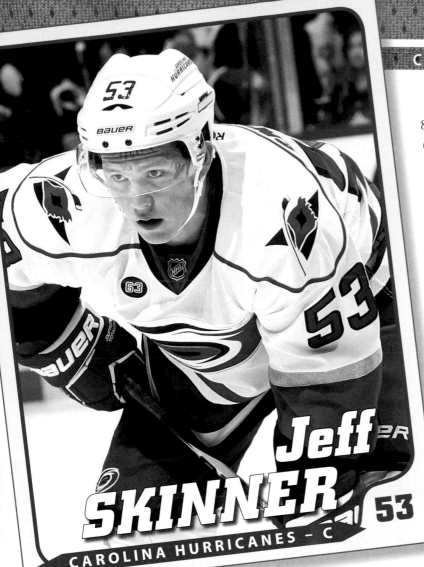

Jeff
SKINNER 53
CAROLINA HURRICANES – C

82 games and led the rookies overall in points with 63 (31 goals and 32 assists). For his efforts, the native of Markham, Ontario, was named the winner of the Calder Memorial Trophy as the best rookie in the NHL for the 2010–11 season.

Skinner is definitely not the biggest player in the league and his listing at 5-foot-11 and 193 pounds seems generous. He is sturdy, though, and he has superior skating skills that don't rely on speed alone. Skinner developed his skating techniques when he was enrolled in a figure skating program at the age of six, and his moves became purely instinctual after hours and hours of practice. He was actually such a good figure skater that he won a bronze medal at the Canadian Junior Figure Skating Championships when he was 12 years old.

Despite the dedication it took to be the figure skater he was, Skinner still found time to play organized hockey, even though it was never his stated goal to make it to the NHL. Former Toronto Maple Leafs star Rick Vaive coached Skinner when he was 15 years old and playing with the Toronto Young Nationals. Vaive recalls that Skinner showed great balance on his skates even though his skating was not exactly smooth. He also realized that Skinner was a natural goal scorer after he scored 65 goals in 56 games for the Nationals in 2007–08. These goal-scoring skills made Skinner a standout when he joined the Ontario Hockey League's Junior A Kitchener Rangers for the 2008–09 season.

Two years in Kitchener saw Skinner score 77 times in 127 games and he totaled 141 points. These numbers put his name in the discussion as one the better players available in the 2010 draft, but there were still lingering doubts about his foot speed. Scouts were concerned about how Skinner would fare among the bigger and faster NHL players, but, at the same time, knew he had a knack for breaking away when he had a chance to snare a loose puck.

Skinner reported to his first pro camp in excellent

The talk in the lead-up to the 2010 NHL entry draft focused on two players — Taylor Hall and Tyler Seguin — and it was easy to understand why, since both were extremely talented and expected to make the final roster of the NHL teams that selected them. In the end, the Edmonton Oilers selected Hall first overall and the Boston Bruins took Seguin with the next choice. Typically, the remaining picks in the top 10 net excellent players, but to get an NHL-ready prospect is never a certainty. For the Carolina Hurricanes, however, such was the case when they selected center Jeff Skinner with the seventh overall pick in the 2010 draft.

Not only did Skinner make the Hurricanes' opening-day roster, but over the course of the entire season he outperformed Hall and Seguin as he suited up for all condition and he produced the most offense at even strength for the 2010–11 Carolina club, recording 25 goals and 20 assists. He also became the youngest player in the NHL to appear in the All-Star Game after he demonstrated a nice pair of soft hands and the skills that were necessary to get his stick free and clear in order to snap off his good shot. Unfortunately, the Hurricanes finished the season out of the playoffs, but they did have a winning season with a 40–31–11 record.

The second season for any NHL player is always more difficult, and Skinner was no exception to the rule. He missed a number of games in 2011–12 with a concussion, but he still scored 20 goals and racked up 44 points in just 64 games.

At this point in his career, the sky is truly the limit for the former figure skater who, at 20 years old, has already shown he has a grasp of the NHL game. Skinner is one of the best young players in the game and the Hurricanes have a solid opportunity to use him as a building block in the years to come.

- ➤ Drafted 7th overall by the Carolina Hurricanes in 2010
- ➤ Played in the 2011 NHL All-Star Game
- ➤ Won the Calder Memorial Trophy as the top rookie for the 2010–11 NHL season
- ➤ Selected to the NHL's All-Rookie Team in 2011
- ➤ Recorded 107 points (51 goals and 56 assists) in 146 career games

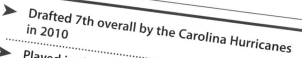

CAREER HIGHLIGHTS

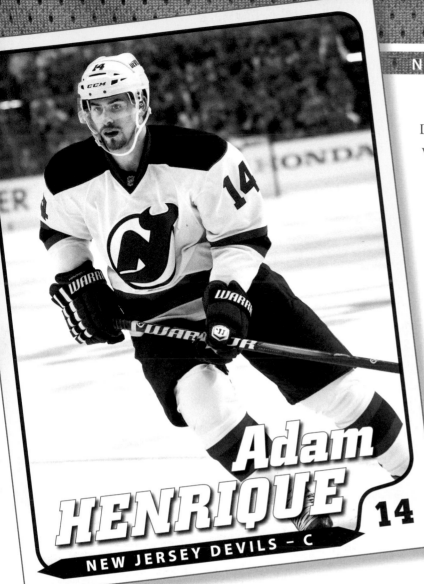

Adam HENRIQUE 14

NEW JERSEY DEVILS – C

For a young man of just 22 years old (and one who is in his first NHL season), New Jersey Devils center Adam Henrique has certainly shown a flair for the dramatic. During the 2012 Stanley Cup playoffs, Henrique showed his penchant for scoring big goals at the NHL level — he scored the Game 7 double-overtime winner versus the Florida Panthers to get his team into the second round, and the goal was actually Henrique's second of the game. On the winning tally, Henrique grabbed a loose puck in the Florida end and moved into the middle of the ice before firing a low drive that beat veteran Jose Theodore in the Panthers' net. The entire arena was stunned and the Panthers were shocked to lose at home in the last game of the series. The drama was just starting for Henrique and the happy

Devils who mobbed the youngster after his game-winning goal.

After beating the Philadelphia Flyers in the second round, the Devils had to face their division-rival New York Rangers in the Eastern Conference final. The series went back and forth but the Devils had a chance to eliminate the Rangers on home ice in Game 6. The game went into overtime and it was Henrique who was at the right spot to jam a loose puck past New York netminder Henrik Lundqvist to give the Devils a 3–2 win. Henrique jumped up into the glass and his joyous team-mates once again climbed all over the overtime hero. Henrique's second overtime winner put the Devils into the Stanley Cup final against the Los Angeles Kings, but the Devils quickly fell behind 3–0 in the series. Further, Game 4 was played in Los Angeles, but Henrique helped to spoil the Kings' party by scoring the winning goal late in the third period to give the Devils their first win of the series. New Jersey won one more game before the Kings took the Cup on home ice during Game 6. Henrique, however, totaled 13 points (5 goals and 8 assists) in 24 playoff games and made himself a well-known player by the time the 2012 postseason was over.

Henrique was born in Brantford, Ontario, in 1990, but was raised in the nearby farming community of Burford. He caught the attention of the Windsor Spitfires while he was playing in Brampton and he started his Ontario Hockey League (OHL) career as a 16 year old in 2006–07. In four seasons with the Spitfires, Henrique recorded 228 points (including 111 goals) in 238 games and he was on a pair of Memorial Cup–winning teams (2009 and 2010).

Henrique, however, is not the largest player in the league (he's listed at 6-feet, 200-pounds), and his size might the be reason he was available late in the 2008 NHL entry draft. He was taken 82nd overall by the Devils, a team that has a reputation for making good choices deep in the draft. The Devils let the youngster

finish his junior career and then assigned him to the Albany Devils of the American Hockey League for the 2010–11 season that saw him score 25 goals and add 25 assists in 73 games. The following season, he was more than ready to play another year in Albany, but an early-season injury to the Devils' Travis Zajac gave Henrique a chance to show what he could do at the big-league level. In 74 games Henrique tallied 16 goals (4 were short-handed) and 51 points while playing over 18 minutes per game. His impressive play earned him a nomination for the Calder Memorial Trophy as best rookie of the 2011–12 season.

When it comes down to it, Henrique is an excellent two-way player, which is the type the Devils love to have on their team. Overall, Henrique is a great skater with a strong first stride, and he also knows how to put his excellent shot on net. He's certainly not a tough player (he only has seven penalty minutes), but he does hit hard and shows no fear. Henrique worked hard on his strength and all-round game

during his junior days and all his efforts have paid off in the NHL — his skill set will keep him in the league for many years to come and he will undoubtedly be a large part of the rebuilding of the Devils, a team that will be relying on many of its youngsters in the years to come.

- ▶ Drafted 82nd overall by the New Jersey Devils in 2008
- ▶ Member of two Memorial Cup–winning teams with the Windsor Spitfires
- ▶ Scored 25 goals as a rookie in the AHL
- ▶ Named to NHL's All-Rookie Team in 2012
- ▶ Recorded 16 goals and 51 points in 75 career games

CAREER HIGHLIGHTS

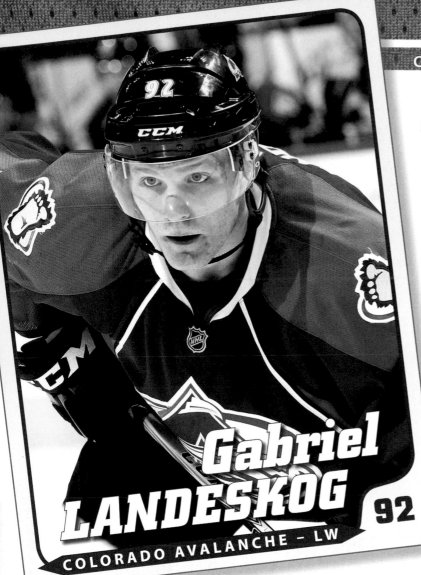

Gabriel LANDESKOG 92

COLORADO AVALANCHE – LW

Elite League, recording 22 points in 23 games. In the spring of 2009, Landeskog was named the captain of Sweden's under-18 team that went on to finish in fifth place at the World Under 18 Championships held in Grand Forks, North Dakota.

In the fall of 2009, Landeskog joined the Kitchener Rangers, and the team's coach and general manager Steve Spott took an immediate liking to him. That season, Landeskog racked up 46 points (24 goals and 22 assists) as an OHL rookie and just one year later was named the first European captain in the 48-year history of the franchise.

Following this achievement, Landeskog was named to Sweden's entry at the 2011 World Junior Championships being hosted in Buffalo, New York. He played just one game, collecting a goal and an assist, before being sidelined for the rest of the tournament with a high ankle sprain. The injury shortened Landeskog's season with Kitchener to just 53 games, but he still led his team with 36 goals.

At the 2011 NHL draft in Minnesota, the consensus first overall pick, Ryan Nugent-Hopkins, was scooped up by the Edmonton Oilers. The Colorado Avalanche, drafting second overall, their highest position since relocating from Quebec City 16 years earlier, were ecstatic to draft Landeskog, who was ranked second among North American skaters by NHL Central Scouting. And, just like he had in Kitchener, Landeskog made an impression on Avalanche coach Joe Sacco, landing himself a roster spot with the big club rather than returning to the Rangers. It only took three games for Landeskog to score his first NHL goal, deflecting a shot past Steve Mason of the Columbus Blue Jackets, which was a move that made Landeskog the youngest Swedish player to have scored in the NHL.

In January 2012, Landeskog was the lone Avalanche participant during the NHL All-Star weekend and was named as one of 12 rookies to compete in the Skills Competition. Additionally, by the end of Landeskog's freshman year, he was the only Colorado skater to play

G abriel Landeskog was born in Sweden, but it seems as though the 6-foot-1, 204-pound left-winger has been preparing to play hockey in North America for most of his life. He started learning English in his early school years, and when he had a chance to stay in his native country to play junior hockey, he opted instead to go to Canada to suit up for the Ontario Hockey League's (OHL's) Kitchener Rangers. It proved to be a wise choice and one that certainly helped him get into the NHL much sooner than he might have anticipated.

Landeskog is a hockey prodigy who gives his father Tony a great deal of credit for his love of hockey (Tony played professional hockey in Sweden). Case in point: in the 2007–08 season, when Landeskog was just 15 years old, he made his debut for Djurgården of the Swedish

in all 82 games. His output of 22 goals and 52 points earned him a Calder Memorial Trophy for being the league's best rookie, as he beat out fellow candidates Ryan Nugent-Hopkins of the Oilers and Adam Henrique of the New Jersey Devils.

Landeskog's season was capped off with an invitation to join Sweden at the World Championships, which were being cohosted by his home country and Finland. Landeskog's leadership qualities were once again on display as he was named an alternate captain along with the Detroit Red Wings' Henrik Zetterberg (veteran Daniel Alfredsson of the Ottawa Senators wore the "C").

It has been years since a Swedish-born forward established himself as a franchise player. Daniel and Henrik Sedin — selected by Vancouver in the 1999 draft — are arguably the most recent superstars from Sweden to play up front. The next wave of offensive

Swedish talent includes players such as Loui Eriksson of the Dallas Stars (a consistent scorer and one-time Lady Byng Memorial Trophy nominee), Magnus Paajarvi of Edmonton and Oliver Ekman-Larsson of the Phoenix Coyotes. Landeskog, however, may emerge as the best of the bunch, and if his rookie season is any indication, he might be the next star forward that young players from Sweden are trying to emulate.

Jake
GARDINER 51
TORONTO MAPLE LEAFS – D

solid rookie season, he struggled to stay in the lineup in subsequent years. Finally, in the 2012–13 off-season, he was dealt to the Philadelphia Flyers.

This brings fans to the case of Gardiner. Acquired in a trade between the Maple Leafs and the Anaheim Ducks on February 9, 2011, it was expected that the U.S.-college-trained Gardiner would spend the majority of the 2011–12 season in the minors with the Toronto Marlies of the American Hockey League. The Leafs already had plenty of capable defensemen on the roster, so it only made sense to develop Gardiner slowly and let him become accustomed to the pro game. His performance at the Leafs' training camp in September 2011 made the Leafs change their minds. The smoothness of his game made then-coach Ron Wilson believe that the 21-year-old, 6-foot-1, 173-pound Gardiner was ready for the NHL. Also helping Gardiner's cause was the unfortunate Keith Aulie, another young rearguard who had played well for the Leafs in the last half of the 2010–11 season, but who was assigned to the Marlies while Gardiner was chosen to stay with the Leafs. (Aulie later followed in the footsteps of his predecessors when he was traded prior to the 2011–12 trade deadline.)

If Gardiner's development record is examined, it's easy to see why he was so highly sought after. He had an excellent high school career at Minnetonka High School in Minnesota, during which he was team captain of a squad that won a gold division Schwan Cup tournament title. He was also part of the under-18 American team that competed at the Ivan Hlinka Memorial Tournament in Europe. This enviable résumé helped Gardiner to be selected 16th overall by the Anaheim Ducks in 2008, but the native of Deephaven, Minnesota, decided to attend the University of Wisconsin-Madison for the 2008–09 season. In his first year in the NCAA, Gardiner posted 24 points (3 goals and 21 assists) in 39 games, and in 2009–10, his totals jumped to 10 goals and 31 assists for 41 points. That season, he also played

The Toronto Maple Leafs' track record is not great when it comes to their development of young defensemen. Leafs fans only need to think back to players like Gary Nylund, Al Iafrate and Luke Richardson, all of whom were highly drafted and had good careers in the NHL, but none of whom ever reached his perceived maximum potential. More recent examples are players such as Drake Berehowsky, Kenny Jonsson and Carlo Colaiacovo, who were each considered to be promising Leafs blue-liners. And despite glimpses of excellence, all three players were quickly traded after they didn't develop at the pace the Leafs expected them to.

Now, consider the plight of Luke Schenn. Drafted fifth overall in 2008, the Leafs refused to return Schenn to the junior level for development, and while he had a for the American team that won gold at the World Junior Championships, where he collected 13 points.

Gardiner's game is all about his ability to handle the puck while under pressure. He is a gifted skater and can spin and turn with ease. One of his best attributes is knowing when to join the rush, his work on the power play is impressive, and by the end of the 2011–12 season, Gardiner had scored 7 goals and added 23 assists for 30 points in 75 games. Sure, his defensive-zone work needs improvement, but he was only a minus 2 on the season, which is an impressive mark for a rookie defenseman on a defensively weak team that also struggled in goal.

Gardiner's offense from the blue line and his slick skating skills are highly valued in the NHL, and he is a hot commodity to any team looking to make a deal with the Maple Leafs. It will

therefore be interesting to see if Toronto decides to keep the youngster with the star potential or if the team will divest its interests, like it has done so many times before.

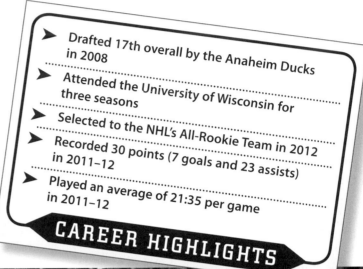

- ➤ Drafted 17th overall by the Anaheim Ducks in 2008
- ➤ Attended the University of Wisconsin for three seasons
- ➤ Selected to the NHL's All-Rookie Team in 2012
- ➤ Recorded 30 points (7 goals and 23 assists) in 2011–12
- ➤ Played an average of 21:35 per game in 2011–12

CAREER HIGHLIGHTS

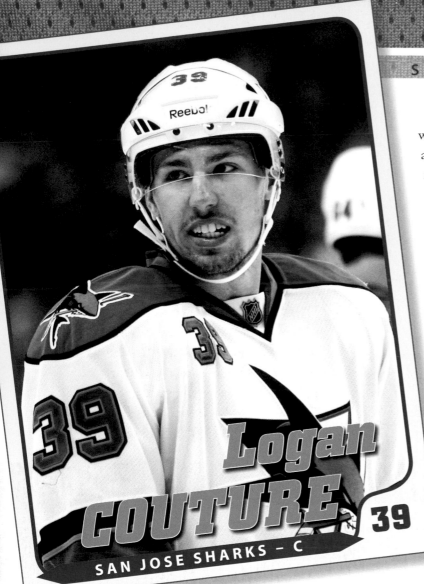

Logan
COUTURE
39
SAN JOSE SHARKS – C

winger Mark Bell. Wilson then went back to the Blues and offered them two of the Toronto selections for the ninth overall draft choice.

The ninth selection of the 2007 draft turned out to be Logan Couture, a 6-foot-1, 195-pound point producing center who had enjoyed an excellent junior career with the Ottawa 67's of the Ontario Hockey League (OHL) — a team Wilson had played with many years ago. The Ottawa club was coached at the time by Brian Kilrea, a man who also mentored Wilson over the course of his long and illustrious career behind the 67's bench.

It is quite likely that Kilrea gave a good recommendation for Couture and that may have helped sway Wilson to move up to grab the promising prospect. The Sharks let Couture play two more seasons in the OHL, where he ended up with 111 goals in 232 games, before he moved to the Worchester Sharks of the American Hockey League for the 2009–10 season. Couture was so good in Worchester, scoring 20 goals and 53 points in his first 42 games, that the Sharks promoted him to the NHL for the last 25 games of the 2009–10 season. Technically, Couture's rookie season on the books is counted as the 2010–11 season, as a player under the age of 26 must play more than 25 games to be considered for Rookie of the Year voting (Couture played exactly 25 games in 2009–10). Couture had a very good 2010–11 with 32 goals — the second best mark on the team — and 56 points in 79 games. Even more impressive was that 22 of his goals came at even strength, while eight of his tallies were game winners. He was also a plus 18 on the season; yet he narrowly missed winning the Calder Trophy to Jeff Skinner of the Carolina Hurricanes.

Couture was selected to the All-Rookie Team at the end of the 2010–11 season. Couture also performed well in the playoffs, scoring seven goals and adding seven assists in 18 post-season games for a team that won two rounds before being eliminated by the Vancouver

San Jose Sharks general manager Doug Wilson is not one to sit idly by and watch his team underperform. He is very willing to trade players and shake up his team in the hopes of finding the right mix. He also understands the value of moving up in the draft to select a player he really wants to add to his team. By the time the 2007 draft took place in June, Wilson had made two deals to secure the ninth overall selection. First, at the 2006–07 trade deadline, he sent a No. 1 draft choice (which ended up being the 16th overall pick) to the St. Louis Blues to acquire veteran winger Bill Guerin. Then he reeled off a trade with the Toronto Maple Leafs that saw San Jose obtain three draft choices — the highest being the 13th overall selection — by sending to Toronto goalie Vesa Toskala and troubled

Canucks in the Western Conference final. What could Couture do for an encore?

The answer to that question came at the end of the 2011–12 season, when he finished with 31 goals and 66 points — second on the team to captain Joe Thornton's 77 points. Couture showed no sign of having any of the problems many NHL sophomores face, but the Sharks were not nearly as successful a club, losing in the first round of the 2012 playoffs in five games to the St. Louis Blues. Couture recorded four points, but it wasn't enough to save the struggling San Jose team.

Sharks coach Todd McLellan loves to play Couture in all situations, as he is such a competitive and composed player despite being just 22 years old. And Wilson has already rewarded Couture for his good play with a two

year $5.75 million contract, which will keep him with the Sharks at least until the 2013–14 season. His teammates consider him a natural goal scorer and a clutch performer, and the latter is something the Sharks have been lacking in recent years — perhaps some of the Shark's veterans can take a page from Couture's book.

Jordan
EBERLE
EDMONTON OILERS – C
14

soil in Ottawa, Ontario, the Canadian team was facing a lot of pressure to win its fifth straight gold medal. Coach Pat Quinn led his roster of teenagers into the semifinal against Russia, and the fans who filled a sold-out Scotiabank Place were treated to an epic matchup. Russia was leading 5–4 heading into the final minute of the game, and as precious seconds ticked off the clock, John Tavares directed a backhand shot toward the Russian goal. The puck was blocked by defenseman Dmitry Kulikov, but it was still loose. Eberle — a right-handed shot — collected the puck and from his forehand to his backhand, deked across the top of the crease and deposited the puck into the net behind Russian goalie Vadim Zhelobnyuk with only 5.4 seconds remaining.

A scoreless overtime resulted in a shootout, and in true storybook fashion, Eberle completed the comeback with the shootout winner. Canada's berth in the gold-medal game was secure, and the team handed Sweden a 5–1 defeat to claim a fifth consecutive title. Eberle registered a remarkable 6 goals and 13 points in 6 games, with his goal in the dying seconds of the semifinal holding up as the tournament's signature moment. Eberle was invited to return to the World Junior Championships the following year, and he compiled eight goals to bring his overall career tournament total to 14, which was a Team Canada record.

To put the exclamation point on his junior career, Eberle finished the 2009–10 season with 50 goals and 106 points in only 57 games for the Western Hockey League's (WHL's) Regina Pats. His performance earned him Player of the Year honors in the WHL as well as within the entire Canadian Hockey League. The Pats, however, didn't make the playoffs that year and Eberle was available to play for the American Hockey League's Springfield Falcons and on Team Canada at the World Championships.

At the Edmonton Oilers' home opener on October 7, 2010, the NHL had its first taste of the 6-foot,

Nothing captivates a global hockey audience like a game between two fierce international rivals. Most Canadians can remember with precision where they were when Paul Henderson, Mario Lemieux or Sidney Crosby scored their famous winning goals for Canada. Just the same, most Americans can tell you what they were doing during the 1980 "Miracle on Ice." But in Canada this passion for hockey extends to the junior level too, and these young players have their own special place in the hearts of Canadian hockey fans. In fact, before Jordan Eberle ever played his first NHL game, the Edmonton Oilers forward cemented his place in Team Canada hockey history by becoming the star of the 2009 World Junior Hockey Championships.

Because the tournament was being hosted on home

185-pound Eberle. His professional career was still in its infancy, but Eberle made his mark with a highlight-reel goal that took the crowd and the rival Calgary Flames by storm. Streaking down the right side, Eberle performed a forehand-to-backhand toe-drag move around the sprawling Flames defenseman Ian White before raising the puck past Calgary goalie Miikka Kiprusoff.

Eberle's rookie season in 2010–11 resulted in 18 goals and a second invitation to join Team Canada at the World Championships. The following year, at just 21 years old, Eberle established himself as a bona fide NHL sniper. Together with Edmonton's Taylor Hall and Ryan Nugent-Hopkins, Eberle is part of a dynamic, young trio that represents the future of the Oilers franchise.

At the end of the 2011–12 season, Eberle's 34 goals, 10 power-play markers and 76 points were good for 15th place overall in each of the three categories. And, in picking up just 10 penalty minutes along the way, he received recognition for his sportsmanship by being named a finalist for the Lady Byng Memorial Trophy.

CAREER HIGHLIGHTS

- Drafted 22nd overall by the Edmonton Oilers in 2008
- Named CHL Player of the Year in 2010
- Played in 2012 NHL All-Star Game
- Scored 34 goals in 2011–12 for the Oilers
- Recorded 52 goals and 119 points in 147 career games

And for the third straight year, Team Canada also called for Eberle to suit up at the World Championships.

The Oilers' rebuilding process has been structured around retaining their first-round draft picks and developing their selections within their organization, even if their short-term success in the standings is sacrificed. But, given the enormous talent of their young stars Nugent-Hopkins, Hall and Eberle, a return to the postseason for Edmonton will likely not be too far into the future.

PROFILE INDEX

ACKNOWLEDGMENTS

Special thanks goes to researcher Rob Del Mundo and to everyone at Firefly Books for their help in creating this book. I'd also like to acknowledge copyeditors Carla McKay, Beth Zabloski and Nicole North, as well as designer Kimberley Young. As always, thanks to my wife Maria and my son David for their support and understanding.

Many media sources were consulted while writing this book, they are:

NEWSPAPERS
Toronto Star, Toronto Sun, Globe & Mail, New York Times, Ottawa Sun, National Post, Montreal Gazette, as well as stories from the *Canadian Press* and the *Associated Press.*

MAGAZINES
Sports Illustrated, Sportsnet Magazine, The Hockey News, McKeen's Hockey Yearbook 2011-12, Maclean's, Breakout.

WEBSITES
TSN.ca, Sportsnet.ca, TheHockeyNews.com, TheFourthPeriod.com, Canoe.ca, Faceoff.com, Hockey-Reference.com, as well as NHL.com and its network of websites.

RECORD BOOKS
NHL Official Guide and Record Book 2012

TELEVISION
Hockey Night in Canada, The NHL on TSN, as well as games broadcast on Sportsnet and the NBC Sports Network.

RADIO
Games broadcast on AM 640 (Toronto), as well as interviews and opinion on TSN radio 1050 AM (Toronto) and on Sportsnet 590 The Fan (Toronto).

BOOKS
Young Guns 2 by Ryan Kennedy and Ryan Dixon (Published Transcontinental Books, 2011).